EXPLORING BRITAIN'S
CASTLES

AA

Editor
Donna Wood

Designer
Andrew Milne

Picture Researcher
Lesley Grayson

Image retouching and internal repro
Jacqueline Street

Cartography provided by the Mapping Services Department of AA Publishing

Contains Ordnance Survey data © Crown copyright and database right 2011

Production
Stephanie Allen

Produced by AA Publishing

Published by AA Publishing (a trading name of AA Media Limited, whose registered office is Fanum House, Basing View, Basingstoke RG21 4EA; registered number 06112600).

A04542

The contents of this book are believed correct at the time of printing. Nevertheless, the publishers cannot be held responsible for any errors or omissions or for changes in the details given in this book or for the consequences of any reliance on the information provided by the same. This does not affect your statutory rights.

Printed in Dubai by Oriental Press

theAA.com/shop

OPENING TIMES

We have given a general guide to opening times within this book, but please be aware that many of the castles, especially those that are privately owned and run, reserve the right to change their opening times without warning.
We therefore strongly advise that you always telephone and/or consult the castle's website before travelling.

Right: Arrow slit in the wall of Arundel Castle

EXPLORING BRITAIN'S
CASTLES

INTRODUCTION

A castle is defined as a 'properly fortified military residence'. In medieval times, the castle was home not only to the owner and his family, but also to his retinue; it was specially designed as the centre of his military operations and to protect him from his enemies. This was a product of feudalism, whereby the lord of the castle agreed to protect his vassals and provide land, while his vassals worked the land and could be called upon for military duty.

British castles tended to come in two basic types – the fortified enclosure and the fortified tower – and sometimes a combination of both. Castles like Framlingham in Suffolk and Dunstanburgh in Northumberland comprised strong walls (with towers) forming an enclosure. This would have been filled with buildings, and, in times of danger, people living outside the castle could take refuge there. An example of a fortified tower, or 'keep', is Hedingham in Essex, a vast multi-storeyed castle with immensely thick walls.

As castles grew larger, owners realized it was impractical to try to squeeze all their worldly goods, livestock and vassals into one tower, and so extra towers and walls were built. This was the origin of great castle complexes like the Tower of London or Dover. In the 12th century, powerful gatehouses were built into the walls to provide an additional layer of protection. In some cases, the gatehouse was even further fortified with walls and ditches, forming what is known as a 'barbican'. Such an arrangement can be seen at Goodrich in Herefordshire, and Conwy had a barbican at each end.

Historians do not agree about whether there were castles in Britain before the Norman Conquest. Obviously the kings and barons of the Dark Ages must have had some kind of strongholds, but their precise structures are not known. After William the Conqueror invaded England in 1066, he needed to consolidate what he had gained and he did this by building simple castles known as 'motte and bailey' castles. The mottes were mounds of earth with flattened tops upon which wooden castles were built, sometimes surrounded by wooden pallisades or fences to form an enclosure (a bailey). Great ditches and banks called 'earthworks' were constructed to provide additional protection, and these can still be seen at Castle Rising and Castle Acre. Later, the wooden pallisades were converted to stone, at many places forming small enclosure castles called 'shell keeps', of which Restormel and Clifford's Tower in York are among the best examples.

Once the Normans had established a hold in Britain, more permanent structures became necessary. Within a few years of William's invasion, building in stone rather than wood was started in castles like Chepstow, Rochester, Colchester and, of course, the great Tower of London. Most of these early castles were simple towers, although Colchester and the Tower were – and still are – impressive for their size and quality.

Although Norman keeps were designed for defence and intended to dominate a defeated people, they were not all alike. The castle-builders skilfully turned the unique character of each site to their advantage, and keeps were variously rectangular, circular, square, multi-sided and D-shaped. At Portchester, the splendid Norman keep was built inside the walls of an existing Roman fort. Others, like Chepstow, took advantage of natural features such as sheer cliffs, using the added protection they provided to form one or more of the castle's flanks.

Below: Drawing of the Tower of London by Anthonis van den Wyngaerde, c.1543
Opposite: 1 Enclosure design at Framlingham Castle 2 Fortified tower at Hedingham 3 Goodrich Castle, with its barbican 4 Earthworks provided extra protection at Castle Acre 5 The shell keep of Clifford's Tower 6 The early stone structure at Rochester

As methods of attacking castles became more refined, so the castles' protective measures and systems were further developed in attempts to keep the fortifications more or less impregnable. In the 12th century, castle owners became aware that a simple keep, however strong and well built, would not be able to withstand a prolonged attack. They began to construct layers of defences (including 'curtain walls') around the keep in a concentric arrangement, following the example of castle-builders in the Near East. The great walls of Constantinople had repelled the Crusaders, and it seems likely that the Crusaders in turn borrowed this idea from their enemies. Dover was probably the first concentric castle in Britain, followed in the late 13th century by castles such as Beaumaris and Caerphilly.

Vaulted gateways and passages at Brougham Castle, near Penrith

Once the Normans were firmly established in power, castle building proceeded at a more leisurely pace. At later points in history, however, it was necessary for a king to embark on a fast and furious spate of castle raising, for instance during Edward I's campaigns in Wales between 1277 and 1284. The Welsh had not been idle during the previous century, and the sturdy fortress at Dolbadarn is an example of a Welsh-built castle. But Edward's Welsh masterpieces – magnificent, dominating structures such as Caernarfon, Conwy, Harlech and Beaumaris – were the ultimate in defensive design of any castles in Britain, and perhaps in the world. Meanwhile, in Scotland, clan leaders like the Douglases were also building mighty castles, for instance Tantallon, while King Alexander II raised the impressive Kildrummy.

The fortified manor house began to emerge in the late 13th century as a new kind of castle. Such houses were often surrounded by a moat, such as at Bodiam, and although defence was still important, the comfort of the owners was also clearly taken into account. Castles were expensive to build, and only the very rich could afford to do so. While many of these fortified manor houses were small, like that at Acton Burnell, some owners wanted their castles to be elaborately expensive in order to display their wealth and power. The magnificent brick tower at Tattershall is a splendid example of this. It was built by the Treasurer of England in the 15th century, and evidence of his riches positively oozes from the decorative stonework and luxurious chambers within.

Scottish castles developed several distinctive features. The Border country was subject to raids by both the Scots and the English for many centuries after Robert the Bruce had won the Scottish wars of independence. In the 14th century small fortified towers, or 'peles', were built to protect local areas against these raids in northern England, while in Scotland, the distinctive 'tower house' began to emerge. During the next 300 years, some 700 of these tower houses were raised in Scotland, from the early ones at Drum and Crichton, to the splendid culmination of castles like Craigievar and Crathes.

Scottish tower houses had thick walls, battlemented parapets and strong turrets on the corners. Many were given the additional protection of extra walls, called 'barmkins', and ditches and banks. The small doorways were often protected by iron gates called 'yetts'. After around 1500, tower houses were provided with specially designed holes so that guns could be fired from them.

Early castles were more military garrisons than homes, but even so, their occupants had to live, and even the most desolate and inhospitable fortress was expected to have a modicum of comfort. In many rooms there were fireplaces, but since many windows would not have had glass, the stone walls and gaps at the shutters must have made them cold and gloomy places, especially in the winter. Castles would also have been noisy. The lord, his family, servants, soldiers, cooks, grooms and a host of others would have been crammed inside. Privacy was an impossible luxury, even for the lord himself.

Many of the chambers would have had paintings, or perhaps tapestries, to decorate the walls. In most castles, there would have been rushes on the floors, although some wealthy owners might have been able to afford rugs. The heart of the castle was the Great Hall. Meals were eaten there, and some would have used the hall as sleeping quarters after the lord had retired to bed. Later castles often had a 'solar' above the hall – an airy, pleasant room, perhaps the forerunner of the drawing room, where the lord could take his ease away from the bustle of the hall. During the daytime, the large windows would have allowed sufficient light for various household tasks to be performed, like sewing and mending. It is likely that the Lord of Tolquhon used his solar to display his fine collection of books.

It was not easy for attackers to overpower great medieval fortresses designed to repel invaders. Most attackers therefore opted for a siege – a waiting game where the defences of the castle were pitted against the equipment and cunning of the attacking army. It was not unknown for treachery to be employed, as was the case when a Scottish blacksmith deliberately sabotaged Kildrummy Castle, allowing the English to take it.

Defenders might make use of the 'sally port', or back door, to harry the camp of the attackers. They could use war machines (called 'mangonels' and 'trebuchets') to hurl missiles at them and, as long as supplies lasted, keep up a constant shower of arrows. These tactics were employed by Simon de Montfort the Younger when he was besieged at Kenilworth in 1266.

Meanwhile, the attackers could hurl missiles back, use battering rams on the gates, or advance on the castle using the protection of 'belfries' or siege towers. If they could get close enough, attackers could undermine the walls by tunnelling underneath to weaken the foundations. A tunnel at St Andrews was aiming to do just that when it was met with a 'countermine' dug by the castle defenders. Unable to dig further under the castle walls, the attackers were forced to abandon their plan. King John successfully undermined one corner of Rochester's keep, with the aid of 40 dead pigs that he set alight in the tunnel. When the heat from the burning pigs caused the tunnel to collapse, part of the keep also fell, allowing John's troops in.

It is often said that the decline of castles came with the evolution of gunpowder, but it is more likely that the importance of castles declined because of changes in medieval society. The feudal system was no longer in place, and lords of the manor wanted comfortable residences, rather than cold and cramped fortresses. It was expensive to convert these vast medieval buildings, and it was often cheaper to build a new

Medieval life is depicted as part of the colourful tapestry 'The Unicorn is Killed and Brought to the Castle' in the Chapel Royal at Stirling Castle

home. Many castles were abandoned for newer and more luxurious houses. However, some castles, like Windsor, Warwick and Glamis, were never abandoned, and have been almost continuously occupied. Thus elegant palaces rub shoulders with formidable keeps, all encased within medieval curtain walls.

9

SOUTH WEST ENGLAND | 1

Although England and France were often at war during the Middle Ages, there was no systematic building of defensive sites along the south west coast. Vulnerable towns like Dartmouth had to petition the king several times before a royal licence was granted to build a castle to protect the town against raiding pirates in the 14th century. Small gun houses were built around Dorset, Devon and Cornwall, but nothing was built on a major scale until Henry VIII annulled his marriage to Catherine of Aragon in 1533. Afraid of recriminations from Catholic France and Spain, Henry quickly built a string of castles to defend England's shores. His intention was that, along with Pendennis on the west bank, clover leaf-shaped St Mawes Castle would defend the east bank of the River Fal from avenging Catholic armies following the royal declaration that the Church of England and Wales was no longer under Papal authority. However, after all Henry's urgency and expense, the expected attack from France and Spain never materialized.

Further inland in the South West region, marital disharmony again has a part to play in castle history; the most notorious story being the medieval murder of King Edward II, who was disembowelled with a red-hot poker on the orders of his estranged wife Queen Isabella and her lover, Roger Mortimer, while a prisoner at Berkeley Castle in Gloucestershire. It is also thought that King John imprisoned his wife for a while at Corfe Castle in Dorset, which was (up until the time of the Civil War) one of the finest castles in England.

BERKELEY CASTLE Gloucestershire

10 miles (16km) south west of Stroud | Open selected days Apr to end Oct | Tel: 01453 810332 | www.berkeley-castle.com

Secluded Berkeley Castle, near the banks of the River Severn, was the site of one of the most infamous of all medieval murders. By 1327, Queen Isabella and her lover, the powerful baron Roger Mortimer, had wrested the crown from Edward II and were running the country. Edward was taken secretly to Berkeley Castle in April 1327, where attempts were made to starve him to death. Dead animals were also thrown into a pit in his room in the hope that the smell would make him sicken and die. But Edward was a strong man and Isabella saw that more drastic measures were necessary. In September, according to tradition, the unfortunate King was murdered by having a red-hot poker thrust into his bowels. Although the chamber in which Edward is said to have

been imprisoned remains, most of the castle dates from the mid-14th century and has survived essentially unchanged since then. It is a great palace-fortress built around a courtyard. Many of Berkeley's rooms are open to visitors, displaying some beautiful furnishings. One room contains furniture said to have belonged to Sir Francis Drake, while the magnificent Great Hall has a superb timber roof dating from the 14th century. Remarkably, the castle is the oldest building in the country still to be inhabited by the same family who built it.

The gardens at Berkeley are also well worth a visit and specialize in scented plants. Gertrude Jekyll was involved with the planting of the terraces at the turn of the last century, and there is also a bowling green, where Queen Elizabeth I was thought to have played bowls when she stayed at the castle. Additional attractions for visitors include the Butterfly House, which contains rare species as well as the world's largest moth, and the plant centre, which sells unusual plants that have been grown in the castle grounds.

Above and left: Berkeley's seemingly peaceful exterior is belied by the cannon positioned on the battlements

Right: The loftily proportioned Great Hall

CORFE CASTLE Dorset

6 miles (10km) south east of Wareham | Open daily all year | Tel: 01929 481294 | www.nationaltrust.org.uk

Once regarded as one of the finest castles in England, Corfe was reduced during the 17th-century Civil War to the collection of ragged walls and shattered towers that today loom over the small town like broken teeth. After Oliver Cromwell's troops had captured this mighty fortress, it was subjected to an unusually brutal 'slighting', which involved undermining anything that could not be blown up with gunpowder.

Perhaps this ferocity resulted from the fact that during the first siege of Corfe, the attackers had been soundly repelled by Royalist troops under the command of the formidable Lady Bankes. She undertook the defence of the castle in 1643 during her husband's absence, and not only managed to withstand the 500 Parliamentarians and their vast array of weaponry and siege equipment, but forced the army to retreat, leaving 100 of their comrades dead.

The second siege occurred in 1646, conveniently timed when Lady Bankes was away, but the spirited defenders held out again until eventually the siege was broken by an act of treachery, rather than military prowess. A small group of soldiers purporting to be Royalists were welcomed into the castle as much-needed additional manpower,

but the soldiers were, in fact, Cromwell's men and they hastened to open the gates and allow the besiegers in. As soon as Cromwell's forces had taken the last prisoner, orders were given to destroy the castle so that it would never again withstand a siege.

Building first commenced on Corfe in the 1080s, on a natural hill commanding fine views of the surrounding countryside, and several kings contributed to its stone construction. Most notably, King John paid £1,400 for walls, a deep ditch-and-bank defence and his 'gloriette'. Corfe was John's favourite castle, and the gloriette was an unfortified residential block containing lavish accommodation for the King, a chapel and offices. Henry III and Edward I each added more towers and walls, making Corfe one of the strongest and most powerful castles in the country.

Corfe Castle was particularly important to King John – he imprisoned his wife here and, four years later, he used it as a hiding place for his treasure and crown. He also used it as a prison, and 22 French knights were starved to death within its walls. Other notable prisoners kept at Corfe included Robert of Normandy, William the Conqueror's eldest son, who was kept captive for most of his life by his youngest brother, Henry I. Edward II was also imprisoned here before his fateful

Left: Early morning mist shrouds Corfe Castle

DARTMOUTH CASTLE Devon

🦁 **13 miles (21km) south of Torquay | Open daily Apr to end Oct, weekends only Nov to Mar | Tel: 01803 833588 | www.english-heritage.org.uk**

At the mouth of the picturesque River Dart a rocky promontory juts out towards the sea, and on this rock stands Dartmouth Castle – an intriguing collection of military buildings spanning no less than six centuries. The most recent addition is a brick gun shelter built during World War II in anticipation of a German invasion.

A castle was built at Dartmouth in the 14th century, although it was not until the 15th century that the citizens of Dartmouth really began to build their fortress in earnest. It comprised a square tower and a round tower, side by side, moulded to suit the shape of the rock, and is the earliest surviving English coastal castle designed specially for artillery. At the same time, another castle was built opposite Dartmouth at Kingswear, ensuring that no French pirates would be able to penetrate upriver to pillage the wealthy town.

The castle itself saw action in the Civil War, when the town was attacked by Cromwell's forces under Sir Thomas Fairfax. In a blaze of gunfire, Fairfax's men stormed the town, taking it within hours and with remarkably few casualties. The 500 Royalists, who had captured Dartmouth Castle after a siege three years before, surrendered their arms on the following day.

You can reach the castle by taking a very pleasant river-boat trip; the ferry departs from Dartmouth quay and lands you a minute's walk from the castle.

Positioned on the estuary of the River Dart (below), Dartmouth Castle has a brick-built gun shelter (left)

DUNSTER CASTLE Somerset

2 miles (3km) south east of Minehead | Open most days Mar to end Oct | Tel: 01643 821314 or 823004 (infoline) | www.nationaltrust.org.uk

Set in an extremely picturesque location between Exmoor and the sea, Dunster Castle has every outward appearance of an ancient stronghold, with its great towers, turrets and battlements – but in fact these castellations were added in the late 19th century.

The castle was built in 1617 and its original fortifications were destroyed after the Civil War, by order of Oliver Cromwell. Thereafter it continued as a fine mansion and many of its handsome features, including intricately decorated ceilings and a superb 17th-century oak staircase, date from the 1680s when a great deal of restoration work was carried out by Colonel Francis Luttrell.

When it was given to the National Trust in 1976, the property had been in the hands of the Luttrell family since Elizabeth, Lady Luttrell, had bought the Norman castle over 600 years before. Nothing but the 13th-century gatehouse remains of this original building, but the Luttrell history can be traced on a tour of the castle through fine family portraits, a framed genealogy (not entirely accurate) and a display case of items which belonged to the family.

The dining room and stairhall are particularly grand, and although the morning room may lack their style and elegance, it does have wonderful views. The gallery is especially interesting for its leather wall hangings depicting the turbulent love story of Antony and Cleopatra.

Dunster Castle enjoys an unusually favourable climate and many subtropical plants thrive among its beautiful garden terraces, notably a huge lemon tree which bears fruit annually.

Above: The north front of Dunster Castle, which was rebuilt between 1862 and 1872 by Anthony Salvin

Left: The oak staircase installed by Colonel Francis Luttrell in the 1680s. The balustrade, carved from elm, sits between newel posts topped by carved vases

LAUNCESTON CASTLE Cornwall

23 miles (37km) north west of Plymouth | Open daily Apr to end Oct | Tel: 01566 772365 | www.english-heritage.org.uk

King Henry III had a younger brother named Richard. It was, perhaps, an unfortunate twist of fate that made Henry the older of the two boys, for Richard was a skilful politician, a cunning diplomat and was wiser by far than his brother the King. Richard used his considerable talents to make himself one of the richest barons in the country – amassing far more wealth than Henry had ever possessed – and with his wealth came a different sort of power. He was elected King of the Romans, and even tried to secure himself the position of Holy Roman Emperor.

In 1227, Richard was made Earl of Cornwall, and it was he who was responsible for building the fine castle at Launceston.

Launceston is a good example of what is known as a shell keep, which consists of a circular wall with buildings inside. Inside this outer wall Richard built another tower, roofed over the space between the two walls, and added a fighting platform around the outside of the outer wall. After Richard's death in 1272, Launceston declined in importance as a military fortress, and by 1353 it was reported that pigs were endangering its foundations by trampling the moat. Launceston was also used as a prison, and it is believed that the much-persecuted George Fox, the founder of the Quakers, was held here for eight months in 1656.

Visitors can view a display tracing around a thousand years of history with finds from excavations of the site, and there are impressive views of the surrounding countryside from the battlements.

Launceston's ruined 12th-century keep is surrounded by a grassy motte and protective stone ring

NUNNEY CASTLE Somerset

3 miles (5km) south west of Frome | Open access daily all year | Tel: 0117 975 0700 | **www.english-heritage.org.uk**

In 1645 Cromwell's men set up a cannon on high ground near Nunney, preparing to lay siege to a castle which was, at the time, held for Charles I. Almost immediately, a hole was made in the north wall, just above the entrance, and Cromwell's troops continued firing to widen the breach. Two days later the castle garrison surrendered and the Parliamentarian soldiers swarmed into Nunney, looting and removing everything of value. The damaged wall remained standing until 1910, when it collapsed into the moat,

blocking it up. The moat was later cleared, and is fed today by the small stream that runs through the village.

Nunney was built by Sir John Delamere in 1373. By this time, the church had already been built in the best position in the village, and so the castle is sited on a stretch of land that most castle-builders would have rejected as too low. But Delamere was perhaps not so much interested in building a strongly defensible fortress as a splendid palace that would reflect his own rising glory

This picturesque 14th-century moated castle suffered some damage during the Civil War

(he later became Sheriff of Somerset and a Knight of the Shire). It is a roughly oblong building, with round towers at each corner, more reminiscent of a French chateau than an English castle, and is an attractive feature of a delightful village. However, this is an unstaffed site with no visitor facilities. When parking, please be considerate to local residents and other road users.

OKEHAMPTON CASTLE Devon

24 miles (38km) east of Exeter | Open daily Apr to end Sep | Tel: 01837 52844 | www.english-heritage.org.uk

Set among richly wooded hills in the rolling Devon countryside, the size and strength of Okehampton Castle come as something of a surprise. Okehampton's history was relatively uneventful, and the only episode of national significance that occurred here was when one of its owners, Henry, Marquis of Exeter, was executed by Henry VIII for conspiracy in 1539, after which the castle was seized by the Crown and dismantled.

Okehampton Castle is, in fact, one of the largest and most extensive castle ruins in the West Country, and is sadly neglected by tourists. It started as a simple mound, probably before 1070, and a stone keep was erected in the late 11th century. In the early 14th century a second building was added to the keep, with thick walls and fine round-arched windows. At the same time, domestic buildings were raised below the keep, producing an elongated enclosure protected by walls and steep slopes. A gatehouse was also raised, connected to the rest of the castle by a long, narrow tunnel. Many of the buildings are in an excellent state of preservation, and this little-known castle is well worth a visit.

There have been many reports indicating that the castle is haunted, and legend has it that the ghost of Lady Howard and a ghostly skeletal black dog regularly visit the premises.

Okehampton Castle as depicted in a 19th-century engraving (below) and as it is today (right)

POWDERHAM CASTLE Devon

The soaring towers of Powderham recall the age of chivalry in a manner totally appropriate to this most romantic castle. Late in the 14th century the building was constructed by Sir Philip Courtenay, a younger son of the Earl of Devon. The castle was besieged and damaged during the Civil War, rebuilt in the 18th century and further changed by Wyatt in the 1790s. For centuries the Courtenays, though descended from a great historic family, prospered in a cautiously provincial manner, their only claim to notoriety being a youthful friendship between the 3rd Viscount and the wicked writer and art collector William Beckford. An exile in New York and Paris, it was the 3rd Viscount, William Courtenay, who discovered from his son's researches into ancient documents in 1831 that he was entitled to revive the Earldom of Devon, a title the family still holds today.

Powderham bears witness to the changing fortunes of the Courtenays. Its exterior is part medieval castle, part Gothic fantasy. The dining hall, though ancient in appearance, is in fact Victorian, with a splendidly romantic fireplace and coats of arms that proudly trace the Courtenay line back to the 11th century. Among the many other rooms, two are quite exceptional: Wyatt's music room, with a spectacular domed ceiling, and the staircase hall. The stairs themselves are grand and beautifully constructed, but the most amazing feature is the plasterwork. Birds and flowers, a cornucopia of fruit, even garden implements tumble in profusion against a bright blue background. The chapel too is interesting, converted from the grange of the medieval castle, with some fine old timbers in the roof. A castle of many different styles and periods, Powderham is full of delights.

Powderham Castle's largely 19th-century exterior conceals a treasure trove of sumptuous furnishings

ST MAWES CASTLE Cornwall

'We are in a very wild place, where no human being ever visits, in the midst of a most barbarous race.' So wrote an ambassador from Venice in 1506, when his ship was forced to take refuge in Cornwall from a violent storm in the River Fal.

In the 16th century Cornwall was indeed an isolated place, a long way from the seat of government and affairs of state, but by the 1530s, Henry VIII was on the brink of a war with France and Spain because he had divorced his Catholic wife, Catherine of Aragon. It became necessary to fortify England's south coast against a possible invasion, and the River Fal was given two forts to protect it – Pendennis on the west

bank and St Mawes on the east. The castle stands on a low headland on the Roseland Peninsula. Its main building is the keep, shaped like a clover leaf, which was raised between 1540 and 1545, and a great deal of care went into its building. It has more decorative carvings than any of Henry VIII's other coastal forts and was built of good-quality stone. The entire fort is well garnished with openings for cannons and other artillery, and further cannons were located outside the keep, aimed across the river.

Today St Mawes Castle is used regularly as a venue for weddings, and for this reason it is closed to the public on Saturdays between April and September.

St Mawes Castle, built to defend the Cornish coast from hostile ships from France and Spain

ST MICHAEL'S MOUNT Cornwall

½ mile (1km) offshore from Marazion | Open selected days Mar to end Oct | Tel: 01736 710507 | www.stmichaelsmount.co.uk

left, the Mount came into the ownership of the St Aubyn family, and in the late 18th century the family began to look upon the Mount as a more permanent residence.

Undaunted by the fact that the living quarters were not of an adequate size, they set about the construction of a new wing – not an easy task on a great rock that is cut off at every high tide.

The St Aubyns were obviously a force to be reckoned with, however, and the splendid Victorian apartments that they added are as much a testament to their determination as to their good taste. Inside the apartments there are some fine plaster reliefs, beautiful Chippendale furniture and collections of armour and pictures.

This isolated castle (left) is still lived in by the St Aubyn family, as is seen from the well-kept interior (below)

An old Cornish legend claims that in the 5th century some fishermen saw the Archangel St Michael on a ledge of rock on the western side of the Mount, and it has been called St Michael's Mount ever since.

Legends aside, this great rock is a picturesque sight. Perched upon its summit is a castle that has been a church, a priory, a fortress and a private home. It was built in 1135 by the abbot of its namesake, Mont St Michel in Normandy, France, to whom

it had been granted by the Norman Earl of Cornwall. However, the original building was destroyed by an earthquake in 1275.

For all its isolation, the Mount was seen as strategically important whenever there was turmoil in England – the Wars of the Roses, the Prayer Book Rebellion, the Armada and, of course, the Civil War, when it was a Royalist stronghold until it surrendered to Parliament in 1646, and was subsequently taken over as a garrison. When the military

SHERBORNE CASTLE Dorset

On the eastern edge of Sherborne | Open selected days Apr to Nov | Tel: 01935 812072 | www.sherbornecastle.com

Sir Walter Raleigh first saw Sherborne Castle when riding to his fleet at Plymouth and – the story goes – was so enchanted by the view that he tumbled from his horse. Encouraged by a gift of jewellery from Raleigh, Queen Elizabeth put pressure on the owner, the Bishop of Salisbury, to relinquish the estate.

Raleigh first attempted modernizing the old Norman castle, but later switched his attention to a site across the River Yeo. Newly married and already with a son, he planned a home for his family and a refuge from his dangerous, fast life. In the grounds he laid out water gardens and a bowling green, planting trees from the New World, with a stone bench beneath their shade.

Raleigh's life here was unorthodox and there were rumours of black masses in the tower study. Cleared on a charge of atheism, but bored with country life, Raleigh led an expedition up the Orinoco, returning sadder and no richer to the home he loved 'above all his possessions, of all places on earth'.

Since 1617 the Digbys have owned Sherborne Castle, many of them matching Raleigh in bravery and individualism. John, later 1st Earl of Bristol, was given the estate by King James I for his attempts to negotiate a Spanish marriage for Prince Charles.

Sherborne Castle is larger than it was in Raleigh's time, but his square Elizabethan house remains central. Most of the interior was refurbished in the 18th and 19th centuries. The light and airy Gothic library is particularly pretty; other rooms are much grander, designed for entertaining royalty. Many of the fireplaces and elaborate ceilings bear the Digby crest of a heraldic ostrich.

'Capability' Brown's grounds maximize the setting; Raleigh's cedars are still growing and his bench is still a great vantage point.

Sherborne Castle looks every bit as enchanting today as it did in Sir Walter Raleigh's time

SUDELEY CASTLE Gloucestershire

Near Winchcombe, 8 miles (13km) north east of Cheltenham | Open end Mar to end Oct | Tel: 01242 602308/604244 | **www.sudeleycastle.co.uk**

The award-winning gardens and mellow stone walls of Sudeley Castle are steeped in history

Set in deeply wooded countryside, Sudeley Castle incorporates the remains of a medieval castle. Some of 15th-century Sudeley is in ruins, having been slighted by Parliamentary forces during the Civil War, but the banqueting hall, built of mellow stone, the tithe barn and the dungeon tower remain. Henry VIII is believed to have visited the castle with Anne Boleyn in 1532. After Henry's death, it became the home of his widow, Katherine Parr, when she married Sir Thomas Seymour in 1547. Among the large retinue that the Queen Dowager brought to Sudeley was the ill-fated Lady Jane Grey.

After a long period of neglect, Sudeley was bought in 1830 by brothers William and John Dent, from a rich family of Worcester glovers. After their deaths, the castle was inherited by their cousin, John Coucher Dent, whose wife Emma devoted her life to the enrichment of Sudeley. With the help of the architect Sir George Gilbert Scott, who designed the beautiful tomb of Katherine Parr in the church, the house was restored.

Entry to the castle apartments is through the Rent Room, where the agent would have collected the tenants' payments, and the North Hall, which was once the guardroom. This room displays a portrait of Charles I by Van Dyck. In the Queen's Bedroom is the remarkable allegorical painting by Lucas de Heere, *Chudleigh*. Blatantly political, it shows Queen Elizabeth I surrounded by the goddesses of peace and plenty, while, in marked contrast, her predecessor, Queen Mary, is depicted with her husband, Philip of Spain, and Mars, the Roman god of war.

Among the relics of Queen Katherine Parr are her prayer book and a love letter to Seymour accepting his proposal of marriage. From the period of the Civil War, there is a display of armour discovered during excavations, as well as a fascinating letter from Charles I to the freeholders of Cornwall.

Sudeley Castle's gardens were laid out during the 19th-century restoration, with fine terraces and spectacular views over the ancient trees in the Home Park.

TINTAGEL CASTLE Cornwall

2 miles (3km) north of Camelford | Open daily all year | Tel: 01840 770328 | **www.english-heritage.org.uk**

In the winter, ferocious storms whip up around the rugged Cornish coast, wearing away at the rocky peninsula that is home to the scanty remains of Tintagel Castle. Each year parts are swept away, and so what remains today is not what would have existed when Reginald, an illegitimate son of Henry I, first raised his castle here.

Tintagel is traditionally associated with the legend of King Arthur, who, it is said, was conceived here while Merlin waited in a cave underneath the castle. The cave that pierces the thin neck of rock that joins the peninsula to the mainland is still called Merlin's Cave, and it can be visited at low tide. This is a wild and desolate place, where it is easy to imagine the romantic image of the legendary hero, but there is no concrete evidence to support the connection.

About 100 years after Reginald had built his square hall, Richard, Earl of Cornwall, built two more enclosures and raised some walls. The Black Prince built another hall, and there is evidence that yet another was raised over the remains of the previous two. Archaeologically, Tintagel is difficult to understand, and there are foundations of buildings and several tunnels, the purpose of which remains unknown – all adding to the castle's air of mystery.

With its stunning location on one of England's most dramatic coastlines, the castle is surrounded by wonderful walks that form part of the Cornish Coastal Path.

Romantic associations with the wizard Merlin and Arthurian legend abound at Tintagel on the Cornish coast. A more magical and dramatic location for a castle would be hard to imagine

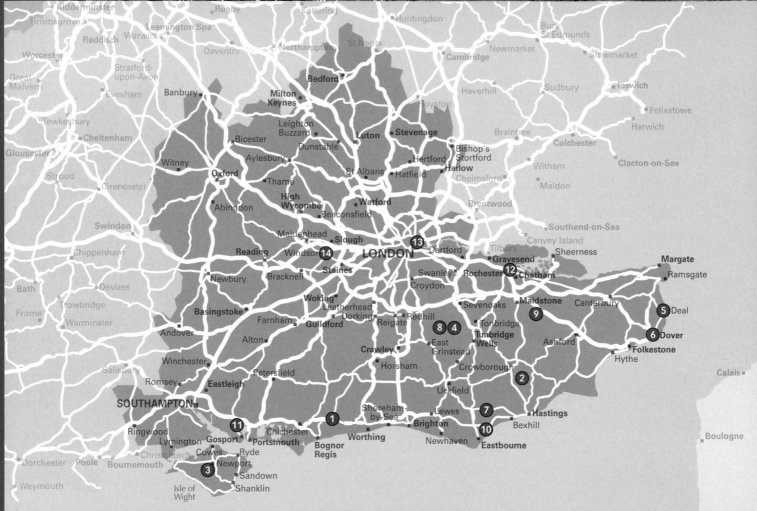

№	Castle	Location	Page
1	**Arundel Castle** West Sussex		32
2	**Bodiam Castle** East Sussex		36
3	**Carisbrooke Castle** Isle of Wight		38
4	**Chiddingstone Castle** Kent		40
5	**Deal Castle** Kent		41
6	**Dover Castle** Kent		42
7	**Herstmonceux Castle** East Sussex		44
8	**Hever Castle** Kent		46
9	**Leeds Castle** Kent		48
10	**Pevensey Castle** East Sussex		50
11	**Portchester Castle** Hampshire		51
12	**Rochester Castle** Kent		52
13	**Tower of London** Central London		54
14	**Windsor Castle** Berkshire		56

SOUTH & SOUTH EAST ENGLAND | 2

Enormous Dover Castle, begun by William the Conqueror, looms over the narrowest point of the English Channel as if issuing a challenge to would-be invaders from foreign shores. Like so many castles in the South and South East of England, it has had a rich and eventful history. Within its grounds are a Roman lighthouse and a beautiful little Anglo-Saxon church. The castle was even used relatively recently, during World War II, to plan the evacuation of Dunkirk.

Deal, one of the 'three castles which keep the Downs', was built by Henry VIII following his denouncement of the Catholic church in 1533. It is a vast sprawling mass of thick stone walls forming six bastions grouped around a single tower, built uncompromizingly for defence. However, the fortunate South and South East region also boasts fairytale castles with graceful towers, soaring spires and waterlily-filled moats, such as Bodiam, Herstmonceux and Arundel, as well as the royal palace-castles of Windsor in Berkshire and the Tower of London, where the Crown Jewels are held.

ARUNDEL CASTLE West Sussex

12 miles (19km) east of Chichester | Open Tue to Sun, Apr to end Oct (also Mon in Aug) | Tel: 01903 882173 | www.arundelcastle.org.uk

In the chapel, marble columns soar upwards to gothic arches and an intriguing striped ceiling, and many of the state rooms contain exquisite furnishings.

In 2008 a new formal garden was opened at Arundel, a lighthearted tribute to the 14th Earl of Arundel (1585–1646), known as 'the Collector Earl' because he commissioned or collected many magnificent works of art, some of which can be seen at the castle. Over the summer there are annual open-air theatre productions in the garden, and visitors may recognize the castle as the setting for many films, including *The Madness of King George* and, more recently, *The Young Victoria*.

Far left: An aerial view of Arundel Castle

Left: Detail of portcullis and arrow slits

Below: 7th Earl of Arundel's tomb in Fitzalan Chapel

Overleaf: Arundel's pale stone battlements

The charming palace-castle, which sprawls among the trees in this attractive West Sussex town, has so many battlemented towers and chimneys that it has an almost fairytale appearance.

There has been a castle at Arundel for some 900 years, ever since a castle mound was raised in about 1088. Around 100 years later, a circular shell keep was built on the mound and, at the same time (or perhaps a little later), Henry II added walls, a chapel and a garden. It is possible that this was the first royal garden in England.

Most of the castle, however, is more recent in construction, and owes much to the work of the 11th Duke of Norfolk, who, in 1787, began to renovate and reconstruct Arundel so that it was fit to become his main home outside London.

Subsequent dukes have continued the renovation work, and today there are many splendid rooms packed with treasures on view to the public. The collection of paintings is especially fine, containing works by such artists as Van Dyck, Lely, Reynolds, Lawrence and Gainsborough.

BODIAM CASTLE East Sussex

12 miles (19km) north of Hastings | Open daily mid Feb to end Oct and selected days the rest of the year | Tel: 01580 830196 | **www.nationaltrust.org.uk**

With its battlemented walls and towers reflected in a moat dotted with waterlilies, Bodiam is one of the most picturesque castles in Britain. But beauty was hardly the prime objective of Bodiam's builder when he constructed his castle and dug his moat – this was a fortress designed to repel invaders and to provide a haven of safety for those lucky enough to be secure within its walls.

Bodiam Castle was built by Sir Edward Dalyngrygge between 1385 and 1388. King Richard II had granted Dalyngrygge a licence to fortify his manor house after the nearby port of Rye had been attacked by the French. Interpreting the licence somewhat more liberally than had been intended, Dalyngrygge promptly abandoned his old manor house and set about building Bodiam Castle.

The castle is rectangular, with a round tower at each corner and a square tower midway along each wall; two of these square towers form gateways. Bodiam is totally surrounded by the wide moat, across which a series of bridges originally gave access to the castle, some at right angles to each other to prevent storming. These elaborate defences against attack were never seriously tested – Bodiam was involved in a skirmish in 1484, but during the Civil War it was surrendered without a shot being fired.

Visitors to the castle can explore battlements and spiral staircases, and get a good impression of medieval castle life, and may, on selected days throughout the year, meet 'real' castle characters in costume. Several events take place, including open-air theatre and a grand medieval weekend.

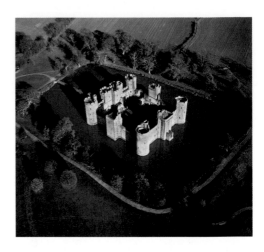

Above: An aerial view of Bodiam Castle shows the wide moat that completely surrounds it

Below: The view across the moat and along the bridge to the gatehouse on the north front

Right: Crests beneath a window at Bodiam

CARISBROOKE CASTLE Isle of Wight

1¼ miles (2km) south west of Newport | Open daily all year | Tel: 01983 522107 | www.english-heritage.org.uk

While a prisoner in Carisbrooke Castle in the summer of 1647, Charles I claimed to his startled supporters that he could escape from his prison because he had tested the size of the bars on the window against his head. What space his head could pass through, the rest of his body, he assured his friends, could follow. After some undignified struggling, Charles was forced to admit that he had misjudged things. Unfortunately for Charles, this was not his only error of judgement, and he was executed in London some 18 months later.

A mound was built here in about 1070, four years after the Battle of Hastings, and a stone shell keep was built on the mound 70 years later. In the 14th century, England feared an attack by the French, and it was at this time that Carisbrooke's spectacular gatehouse was built. French troops did actually manage to land on the island, but the castle was not attacked.

In the 1580s, it was the Spanish who threatened invasion, and the castle was altered and adapted so that it would be able to repel an attack by guns. There are several buildings in the castle courtyard, one of which houses a museum and another which houses the well house.

In 2009 a new, Edwardian-inspired garden was opened within the grounds. Designed by TV gardener Chris Beardshaw, it is in honour of Queen Victoria's daughter, Princess Beatrice, who lived at the castle while she was the Governor of the Isle of Wight from 1896 to her death in 1944. Visitors can also enjoy seeing the famous Carisbrooke donkeys, which demonstrate how water has been drawn up in the well house for hundreds of years.

The entrance gatehouse (left), the King's Bedroom (above) and an aerial view (below) of Carisbrooke

CHIDDINGSTONE CASTLE Kent

10 miles (16km) south west of Sevenoaks | Open selected days Easter to Sep | Tel: 01892 870347 | www.chiddingstonecastle.org.uk

Deep in a picture-book village full of wonderfully preserved Tudor houses, owned by the National Trust and frequently used in period films, lies Chiddingstone Castle. In earlier days it belonged to the Streatfeild family, rich local ironmasters. Henry Streatfeild employed the architect William Atkinson to turn the house into a mock-medieval castle. Atkinson's plans were, in fact, a scaled-down version of Scone Palace in Scotland, which he was building for the Earl of Mansfield, but Henry Streatfeild had overstretched himself financially, and the building work was halted with only the north and south wings completed. However, some cottages were demolished, simply because they spoiled the view, and a lake was installed, which is now popular with anglers. A bream of famously colossal proportions was caught there in 1945.

The Streatfeilds eventually found the house too expensive to keep up and Colonel Sir Henry Streatfeild sold it in 1938. Troops were billeted there during the war, leaving it in a very sorry state, and it was later used as a school. By the time that the late Denys Eyre Bower bought the house in 1955 it was in a bad way. Mr Bower, originally from Derbyshire, had been an obsessive and eccentric collector since his teenage years – all the works of art displayed in the castle today were collected by him. He worked as a bank clerk, but spent so much time collecting antiques that he was first moved to an obscure country branch then finally forced to leave. He set up in London as an antique dealer. Denys Bower died in 1977, leaving everything to the nation, and it was his hope that the castle and contents would be preserved intact – as they have been. There's a portrait of him in the study, along with Chinese porcelain, Derbyshire landscapes, the bust of an Egyptian pharoah and the drawings chest of the great engineer Telford.

Above: The crenellated towers of mock-medieval Chiddingstone Castle

Left: Inside the White Rose Drawing Room

DEAL CASTLE Kent

9 miles (14km) north east of Dover | Open daily Apr to end Sep | Tel: 01304 372762 | www.english-heritage.org.uk

In 1533 Henry VIII, disappointed at not having produced a healthy son, divorced his Catholic wife, Catherine of Aragon. This move not only resulted in Henry being excommunicated, but also brought him in direct conflict with Catholic France and Spain. In order to protect England's southern coasts, Henry built a series of forts, financed largely from the proceeds of the dissolved monasteries.

Deal and nearby Walmer are two of these forts – both plain, functional buildings, where the sole purpose was defence. At Deal, six semicircular bastions are joined to form a tower, which is further protected by an outer wall of the same shape. All were liberally supplied with gun loops and cannon ports, so that, in all, an attacker faced five tiers of guns. Walmer has a simpler plan, involving a circular tower and a quatrefoil outer wall, but the defensive principle is the same, and from every angle an invader would face a bristling armoury of handguns and cannon.

As it happened, Henry's precautions were not necessary and Deal was not attacked until 1648, when it was held for Charles I in the Civil War. It suffered extensive damage, but was not attacked again until a bomb fell on it during World War II.

For those who enjoy cycling, there is a lovely cycle path linking Deal and Walmer castles along the beachfront.

The vast, clover leaf-shaped mass of Deal Castle

DOVER CASTLE Kent

On east side of Dover | Open daily all year | Tel: 01304 211067 | www.english-heritage.org.uk

Dover Castle is so enormous, and contains so many fascinating features, that it is difficult to know where to start in its description. It was a state-of-the-art castle in medieval times, displaying some of the most highly advanced defensive architecture available. Its strategically vital position at the point where England is nearest to the coast of France has given it a unique place in British history. And it is simultaneously powerful, massive, imposing and splendid.

The castle stands on a spur of rock overlooking the English Channel. The entire site is protected by walls bristling with towers and bulwarks. These include the formidable Constable's Gate, erected in the 1220s, a pair of D-shaped towers that not only served as a serious obstacle for would-be invaders, but provided comfortable lodgings for the castle constables (or, nowadays, their deputies). Outside the walls are earthworks and natural slopes that provide additional defence.

The castle was begun by William the Conqueror, but the great keep was built by Henry II in the 1180s. It is surrounded by yet another wall, studded with square towers and two barbicans. The keep itself is 95 feet (29m) tall, and around 95 feet (29m) across at its base. There are square turrets at each corner, and even at the top of the tower, where the walls are thinnest, they are still an amazing 17 feet (just over 5m) thick. The well is carved into the thickness of the wall, and plunges 240 feet (73m) to reach a steady water supply.

Dover has had a rich and eventful history, and one especially important episode occurred during the last year of the reign of King John (1216). John's barons had been growing increasingly frustrated with him, and had invited Prince Louis, heir to the French throne, to invade England and take over. Louis landed at Dover and laid siege to Dover Castle, which was held by Hubert de Burgh,

a baron loyal to John. Ever since the castle was founded, kings had laid down vast sums of money for its repair and development (notably Henry II and Richard I), and it looked as though this investment had paid off. Louis, it seemed, would be unable to breach Dover's powerful walls. Then the unthinkable happened – the French managed to take the outer barbican and undermine the gate. Despite de Burgh's efforts, Louis was poised to enter the inner enclosure. With fortunate timing, John died, the barons proclaimed allegiance to his successor, Henry III, and Louis went home. Lessons were learned, however, and Henry spent a good deal of money in improving Dover's defences.

Visitors to the castle can venture below ground on a tour of the wonderful medieval tunnels, and see how they were adapted during the Napoleonic War in preparation for a French invasion, becoming the only underground barracks ever built in Britain. The secret tunnels also played a key role during World War II, when they were the nerve centre of the Dunkirk operation, and were further extended during the Cold War. One of the main attractions is the underground hospital. Also within the castle grounds are a Roman lighthouse and a beautiful little Anglo-Saxon church.

HERSTMONCEUX CASTLE East Sussex

8 miles (13km) north of Eastbourne | Grounds open daily mid Apr to end Oct (tours on selected days) | Tel: 01323 833816 | www.herstmonceux-castle.com

Many people will associate the fine brick palace at Herstmonceux with the Royal Observatory, which moved here from Greenwich in 1948. In 1989 the Royal Observatory moved yet again, and in 1993 the castle was acquired by Queen's University, Canada, and became an international study centre where important research work takes place.

It was one of the first castles in England to be built of brick, and the effect is stunning. Its clusters of elegant chimneys and the many towers, all in a pleasing shade of rich red, are reflected in the wide moat that surrounds it, rendering it one of the most attractive castles built in the Middle Ages.

Sir Roger Fiennes was granted a licence to build Herstmonceux in 1441. The fact that the castle was built in a lake afforded some

protection, and the impressive gatehouse presented a formidable array of murder holes and arrow slits with which to give hostile visitors a nasty surprise.

Once the castle had passed from the Fiennes family, it had a sad history of careless owners. In the 17th century, one owner shamelessly ripped the interior of the castle out in order to provide himself with the raw materials to build another house, and a great deal of work has been necessary to restore it to its former grandeur.

Visitors are welcome to walk around the grounds, which contain a beautiful Elizabethan walled garden, many woodland trails and lily-covered lakes. There are also guided tours of the castle, which give an insight into what life was like in times gone by and the various characters connected with the castle, including resident ghosts. Contact the castle for dates and times of tours, as they are not always available.

Left and above: Elegant brick-built Herstmonceux Castle stands in a lily-covered moat

HEVER CASTLE Kent

3 miles (5km) south east of Edenbridge | Open selected days Mar to Dec | Tel: 01732 865224 | www.hevercastle.co.uk

Double-moated Hever Castle is perhaps best known for being the home of the ill-fated Anne Boleyn. There are four crucial periods in its building and family history – the 13th century, the mid-15th and 16th centuries and the early 1900s – and no less than four famous figures dominate Hever's story.

The first is the bewitching Anne Boleyn, second wife of King Henry VIII and the mother of Queen Elizabeth I. Hever Castle was her childhood home. She lived dangerously and died young when the executioner's sword severed her pretty, slender neck in the Tower of London.

The second figure is King Henry himself, who came to Hever to court her. The third is his fourth wife, the distinctly unbewitching Anne of Cleves, to whom he gave the estate. The fourth, 350 years later, is the American multi-millionaire William Waldorf Astor, who rescued Hever from gentle decline and, with admirable taste and judgement and a mountain of money, created the romantically beautiful house and grounds of today.

The oldest part of Hever is the sternly massive gatehouse, which was built in about 1270 and today houses some fascinating instruments of torture and punishment. There was a strong wall around the bailey, or yard, and the whole place was protected by a moat. Nothing else of much importance happened for 200 years or so, until the appearance of the Bullens, or Boleyns.

The Bullens transformed Hever from a crude castle into a comfortable residence, built round a central courtyard. What is now the inner hall, with its rich Edwardian woodwork, was their Great Kitchen. There's a copy of the famous Holbein portrait of Henry VIII, with portraits of both Anne and Mary Boleyn, and the clock on the mantelpiece is a copy of the one that Henry gave Anne as a wedding present. They were wed early in 1533, when she was already pregnant. By this time, she had taken to spelling her surname more grandly as Boleyn, and on 1 June 1533 she was crowned Queen of England in Westminster Abbey.

At Hever are touching mementos of Anne's short life, including embroidery that she worked. In the little bedroom that was hers as a girl are portraits of her and the prayer book that she carried with her to the block on Tower Green. In it she wrote: 'Remember me when you do pray, that hope doth lead from day to day, Anne Boleyn.'

As you proceed round the house, you have to keep mentally switching from the 16th century to the 1900s and back again. The drawing room, morning room and library are wonderfully luxurious Edwardian creations, but at the same time eminently liveable-in today.

Left and right: The childhood home of Anne Boleyn, Hever Castle has a surprisingly cosy atmosphere

LEEDS CASTLE Kent

5 miles (8km) east of Maidstone | Open daily all year | Tel: 01622 765400 | www.leeds-castle.com

Leeds Castle is not, as many would-be visitors might suppose, in the city of Leeds in West Yorkshire, but in the depths of the beautiful Kent countryside. It takes its name from its first owner, a man named Leed, or Ledian, who built himself a wooden castle in 857. Leed was the Chief Minister of the King of Kent, and in a time when a fall from grace or an attack by rival parties was a way of life, Leed was very wise in building a stronghold for his family on the two small islands in the lake formed by the River Len.

It is difficult to imagine what the original Leeds Castle must have looked like, especially when confronted by the grandeur of the building that stands on the two islands today. Edward I rebuilt the earlier Norman castle (which had been erected by one of William the Conqueror's lords in 1119), providing it with a set of outer walls, a barbican, and the curious 'gloriette', a D-shaped tower on the smaller of the two islands, which was altered extensively in the Tudor period. During this time, Henry VIII was

a frequent visitor. Most notably, he came with his queen Catherine of Aragon and their entire court en route to France to attend the legendary tournament of the Field of the Cloth of Gold in 1520.

Much of Leeds Castle was restored and rebuilt in the 19th century. The last private owner of the castle, Olive, Lady Baillie – the daughter of an American heiress and an English lord – embarked on a complete refurbishment, and filled the castle with art and antiques, collected on her frequent buying trips around Europe.

Many of the rooms are open to the public, all lavishly decorated. There are plenty of other attractions at Leeds too, including a yew and a turf maze, an underworld grotto, an aviary, falconry displays, and a fascinating dog-collar museum featuring over 100 historic dog collars. There is also a golf course and, for the more adventurous, a 'Go Ape' high-wire obstacle course as well as hot-air balloon flights available during the summer months.

Olive, Lady Baillie, completely refurbished Leeds Castle (left and below), entertaining princes and politicians there and filling it with works of art. Her collection of shoes (above) is suitably glamorous

PEVENSEY CASTLE East Sussex

4 miles (6km) north east of Eastbourne | Open daily Apr to end Oct, weekends only Jan to Mar | Tel: 01323 762604 | **www.english-heritage.org.uk**

At nine o'clock in the morning on Thursday 28 September 1066, an invading army landed on the English coast. Their leader, William, Duke of Normandy, a veteran of many battles, immediately seized the Roman fort at Pevensey and dug ditches to provide his troops with added protection in the event of an attack. The attack did not come, and William quickly moved his army to a better site along the coast at Hastings, where he erected his first castle.

Once the Battle of Hastings was over, and Duke William became King William, the Normans needed to consolidate their position by building castles and controlling the land around them. William gave Pevensey to his half-brother, Robert of Mortain, who built a castle inside the old Roman fort. Years later, perhaps about 1100, work started on raising a large keep.

The castle has had many owners, and has been besieged on several occasions, notably by William II in 1088, Stephen of Penchester in 1147, and Simon de Montfort the Younger in 1264–65. The last siege is perhaps the most famous. It happened after the Battle of Lewes, in which Henry III was defeated by his barons. The King's supporters took refuge in the town of Pevensey, but Simon de Montfort was unable to take the castle.

Trebuchet balls (below), excavated from the moat at Pevensey Castle (right)

PORTCHESTER CASTLE Hampshire

🦁 **4 miles (6km) east of Fareham | Open daily Jan to end Oct | Tel: 02392 378291 | www.english-heritage.org.uk**

The origins of Portchester Castle stretch much further back in time than its Norman buildings, for Portchester was a Roman coastal fortress constructed in the 3rd century AD. The Roman walls still stand tall and strong today, as they did when the Normans came and built a great keep inside this sturdy fortress.

The Roman fort was a great square enclosure, protected by high walls studded with protective towers. In 1120 the Normans built a fine keep using cut stone imported from Caen in France. Originally, the keep was only two storeys high, but about 50 years later it was given an additional two floors, and 200 years after this Richard II added battlements.

Because of its strategically important position on the coast, several medieval kings spent a good deal of money on maintaining and improving the castle. Richard II is believed to have raised the buildings between the keep and the gatehouse called 'Richard's Palace'. Edward I presented the castle first to his mother and then to his wife. Before the castle came into royal hands, Augustinian canons built a priory in the south-eastern corner of the fort, and their splendid chapel can still be seen by visitors today. The castle grounds are a lovely atmospheric place to have a family picnic.

Right and below: Glorious golden-stoned Portchester Castle was originally a Roman coastal fortress

ROCHESTER CASTLE Kent

10 miles (16km) north of Maidstone | Open daily Jan to end Oct | Tel: 01634 402276 | www.english-heritage.org.uk

The magnificent Norman keep at Rochester has seen more than its share of battles and sieges, but perhaps the most famous was in 1215. Shortly after the barons forced King John to sign the Magna Carta, he turned against them in a bitter war. Rochester Castle was held for the barons, and John laid siege to it with incredible ferocity. The siege lasted for about seven weeks, during which time those in the castle were reduced to a diet of horse meat and water. Meanwhile, John kept a constant barrage of missiles from crossbows and ballistas (stone-throwing machines), and began to dig a tunnel under the keep itself. Part of the keep collapsed, but the defenders bravely fought on. Those who could no longer fight were sent out, where it is said John had their hands and feet cut off. But Rochester finally fell, and the defenders were imprisoned.

Building on the keep started in about 1127, and it is one of the largest in England. Its walls soar to 113 feet (34m) high and are up to 12 feet (3.7m) thick. The well was 65 feet (20m) deep and was cleverly constructed so that fresh water could be drawn up from any of the keep's four floors. Although the keep was first and foremost a defensive building, there are some beautifully carved archways and windows.

In the run-up to Christmas, a Dickensian market brings an air of revelry to the castle. The ancient walls are illuminated in traditional Christmas colours, the trees twinkle with fairy lights and the smell of roast chestnuts permeates the air. Dickensian characters and street entertainers mingle outside the castle walls, while carol singers and bands entertain visitors to the market.

Construction of magnificent Rochester Castle (left and above right) was started as early as 1087, by Gandulf, Bishop of Rochester. Beautiful carving is still visible around the pillars and archways (right and far right)

TOWER OF LONDON
Central London

Tower Hill, EC3 | Open daily all year | Tel: 0844 482 7777 (information) or 7799 (bookings) | www.hrp.org.uk/toweroflondon

Standing proud and strong in the very heart of England's capital city, the Tower of London has had a long and eventful history. It conjures up many images for visitors – beefeaters and ravens, the crown jewels, Traitors' Gate – and a multitude of executions.

William the Conqueror began work on the keep, known as the White Tower, in about 1078, but it was probably completed by William II some 20 years later. Building in the Tower of London complex has continued throughout history, right up to the Waterloo Barracks built in 1845, and the new high-security Jewel House. The variety of the buildings reflects the Tower's use as a royal residence, a prison, the Mint, the Royal Zoo, a public records office, the Royal Observatory and the stronghold for the crown jewels.

The Tower is noted for its bloody history. The first execution here is thought to have been that of Sir Simon Burley, who was beheaded in 1388. Two different places of execution are connected with the Tower: Tower Hill, a patch of land outside the castle walls which was for public executions, and the more discreet Tower Green, inside the

castle in the shadow of the White Tower. In 1465 a permanent scaffold was erected on Tower Hill by Edward IV. Countless heads followed the unfortunate Simon Burley's, including those of Sir Thomas More (1535), the Earl of Essex (1540), and John Dudley, the Duke of Northumberland (1553), and his son Guildford (1554). Tower Green witnessed the execution of two of Henry VIII's wives and the unlucky 16-year-old Lady Jane Grey, executed by 'Bloody Mary' in 1554.

Not everyone detained at the Tower was executed, and famous prisoners who languished within its gloomy walls included Princess Elizabeth (later Queen Elizabeth I), Judge Jeffries and William Penn. But even when not under the threat of execution, prisoners were not necessarily safe. Henry VI was murdered in the Wakefield Tower in 1471, and the boy king Edward V and his brother, the Duke of York, are believed to have been murdered in the Bloody Tower. A number of prisoners attempted an escape – some successfully, like the charismatic Ranulf Flambard, Bishop of Durham, who climbed down a rope smuggled to him in

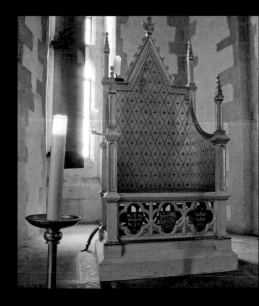

a jug of wine. Others were less fortunate – Gruffudd, the son of Llywelyn the Great, attempted a similar escape, but the rope broke as he climbed down it and he fell to his death. Sir Walter Raleigh and Guy Fawkes were other famous prisoners in the Tower, but they were both executed elsewhere (beheaded in Whitehall and hung, drawn and quartered in Westminster respectively).

The Tower is the scene of some historic ceremonies. Coronations and royal birthdays are celebrated by guns fired from the Tower, but perhaps more famous is the Ceremony of the Keys, carried out as the Tower is locked each night. Tradition has it that if the ravens ever leave the Tower, the monarchy will fall. Today, precautions are taken against such an event, including clipping the ravens' wings and keeping a number of extra ravens to hand, just in case.

Far left: The White Tower, begun by William the Conqueror in about 1078

Left: The portcullis of the infamous Bloody Tower

Above: Reproduction 13th-century Coronation throne in the Wakefield Tower

WINDSOR CASTLE Berkshire

2 miles (3km) south of Slough | Open daily all year | Tel: 020 7766 7304 | **www.royalcollection.org.uk**

Windsor Castle is not only the official residence of HM The Queen, but it is also the largest inhabited castle in the world. The battlemented towers and turrets have been fortress, home and court to English monarchs since the 11th century.

William the Conqueror began work on the castle, raising a simple motte and bailey structure on a chalk cliff. Since then, Windsor has been almost continuously occupied, and many kings changed or added buildings during the next 900 years. Thus Henry II remodelled the great Round Tower, Edward III began to convert the military buildings into a royal residence, Edward IV started (and Henry VIII completed) the elegant St George's Chapel, and Henry VIII added the fine gatehouse. In the 1820s George IV spent a million pounds on modernizing and repairing this splendid medieval fortress. The castle remained virtually unchanged from that time until the devastating fire in 1992, which destroyed parts of the historic buildings, causing millions of pounds' worth of damage.

Windsor was a favourite among kings. Henry I was married here, Henry II planted a herb garden and regarded the castle as home, and Henry III famously entertained the local poor to a great feast here one Good Friday. Edward III was born in the castle, and his Knights of the Order of the Garter later adopted St George's Chapel as their place of worship. The castle withstood two sieges by King John during the Magna Carta Wars.

As a working palace, the castle is used frequently by the Queen for state ceremonies and official entertaining, so opening times, particularly of the state apartments, may change at short notice. Before planning a visit it is essential to check current opening arrangements by phone or via the website.

Crenellation detail (right), a main turret (far right), and the Long Walk entrance through the Great Park (below)

3

WALES & THE MARCHES | 3

Edward Longshanks, who ruled England from 1272 to 1307, was one of the most powerful English kings in history. Determined to put an end to Welsh bids for independence, he built a string of fortresses in Wales. Edward's chief opponent was Llywelyn the Last. Llywelyn's wars with Edward came in two phases, each resulting in a frenzy of castle building on Edward's part. The first confrontations occurred in 1276 and 1277. Llywelyn had married the daughter of Edward's enemy Simon de Montfort and was refusing to pay homage to Edward. The King acted quickly and effectively, driving Llywelyn into his Gwynedd stronghold. Llywelyn had no option but to yield.

In order to consolidate what he had won, Edward employed the great military architect Master James of St George. Edward and Master James constructed castles at Flint and Rhuddlan, and fortified already existing castles at Builth and Aberystwyth. Ruthin and Hawarden were also raised. The sight of these English-built fortresses on Welsh land naturally caused discontent. In 1282, Llywelyn rallied to his people's call for him to lead them against English repression. Edward put down the rebellion even more ruthlessly than before. Llywelyn was killed in an ambush, and, with his death, Welsh resistance began to crumble. Edward stormed into Wales, taking Dolwyddelan, Dolbadarn and Castell-y-Bere. This time, he ensured that no further rebellions could take place, and ordered Master James to design castles at Conwy, Harlech and Beaumaris. Edward's North Wales castles display some of the most splendid military architecture in the world. They are stark symbols of Edward's dominance over a defeated nation, but at the same time, magnificent illustrations of medieval lifestyle.

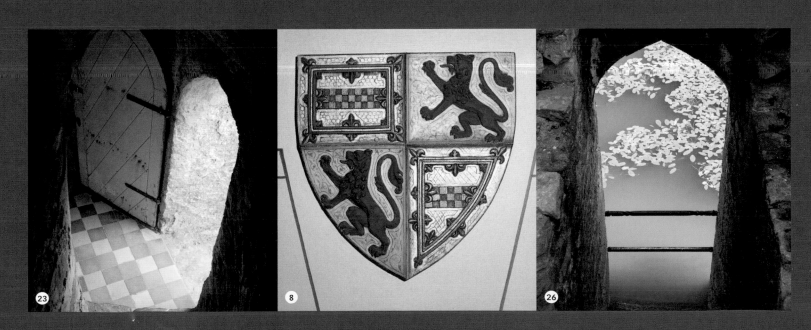

23 8 26

ABERYSTWYTH CASTLE Ceredigion

Overlooking the harbour is the once-mighty castle built in 1277 for Edward I as part of his impregnable 'iron ring', following his first successful campaign in Wales.

Edward I became King of England in 1272 and was crowned two years later in Westminster Abbey. He was a natural military leader and tactician and he set his sights on ruling the whole of the country by conquering Scotland and Wales.

Following his successful campaigns in Wales, Edward recognized Welsh law and government, creating counties in the north of Wales very similar to those that existed in England. He also established boroughs for the English settlers, which the native Welsh were forbidden to enter, although with time and with mixed marriages they soon did. This was also Edward's great castle-building period, when mighty Harlech, Caernarfon and Conwy were built. Aberystwyth, Builth, Flint and Rhuddlan followed.

There has been a castle in Aberystwyth since 1110, when Gilbert of Clare built a castle near the mouth of the River Ystwyth, the hills and ditches of which are still visible. The present castle was located on the coast overlooking the town and took 12 years to complete, but it appears that building standards were poor, as it had to be extensively rebuilt at a cost of several thousand pounds.

The town and castle fell to the Welsh under Owain Glyndwr in 1404 and for a short time Wales had its parliament there. With the demise of Glyndwr, the last Welsh Prince of Wales, however, the castle again came into English hands, later becoming tangled up in English politics. During the Civil War it was blown up and left to disintegrate into the ruins seen today.

Aberystwyth Castle has been in its present ruinous state since the time of the Civil War

ACTON BURNELL CASTLE Shropshire

7 miles (11km) south east of Shrewsbury | Open access all year | www.english-heritage.org.uk

The elegant ruins of Acton Burnell are reached by a short walk from the car park along a wooded path. It is charming, standing among the trees – a quiet, peaceful place, disturbed by little more than the singing of birds. Roofless, with only the walls still standing, it has large windows on the ground floor – an unusual feature, because windows would have been difficult to defend if it had ever come under attack. In times of peace, however, they had the advantage of allowing light into what would otherwise have been a rather gloomy set of ground-floor rooms.

Acton Burnell Castle was originally built by Robert Burnell, after whom it was named. Burnell was an extremely important man during the 13th century, serving both as Edward I's Chancellor of England and as Bishop of Bath and Wells.

Because medieval kings were usually worried about how much power their barons were amassing, no one was allowed to build a castle without the king's express permission. In some cases, the king might give one of his subjects a 'licence to crenellate', which meant that an existing house might be given some defensive features, such as a new tower or battlements. In the 1280s, Robert Burnell was granted such a licence, and Acton Burnell was given a set of battlemented parapets.

A statuesque Cedar of Lebanon (right) looms over the red sandstone ruins of Acton Burnell Castle (above)

BEAUMARIS CASTLE
Isle of Anglesey

🦁 **5 miles (8km) north east of the Menai Bridge | Open daily all year | Tel: 01248 810361 | www.cadw.wales.gov.uk**

Sitting majestically on the shores of the Menai Strait, looking from the island of Anglesey across to mainland Wales, this powerful castle took more than 35 years to build, and even so was never completely finished. It was the last of the great castles built by Edward I following his conquest of Wales, and was designed by Edward's most famous and acclaimed castle-builder, Master James of St George (1230–1308).

The building of Beaumaris Castle was started in 1295, and with its wide moat, high walls and strong towers, the castle was thought to be impregnable. However, this was never put to the test, and no siege machines or artillery have ever been fired at or from the walls of this mighty fortress.

Unfortunately, less than 20 years after building work stopped on the still-unfinished castle, there were reports that it was already falling into decay.

Master James had not intended Beaumaris to be merely a powerful fortress, but had designed it with comfort in mind – the inner buildings had luxurious chambers, with an extensive array of kitchens, stables and a chapel. The castle itself is in two rings, one inside the other. The inner ring has two massive twin-towered gatehouses, while the outer ring is a wall 27 feet (just over 8m) high, bristling with defensive towers and its own protected dock.

An aerial view (below) shows the intricate layout of Beaumaris Castle, with its mighty towers (top left) and domestic buildings that included a chapel (bottom left)

CAERNARFON CASTLE Gwynedd

7 miles (11km) south east of Bangor | Open daily all year | Tel: 01286 677617 | www.cadw.wales.gov.uk

In 1282, Llywelyn the Last, the last native Prince of Wales, was killed in an ambush, and Welsh resistance to English occupation began to crumble. The victorious Edward I offered the Welsh a prince who was born in Wales, could speak no word of English, and whose life and reputation no one would be able to stain. He had in mind his infant son, later Edward II, who became the first English Prince of Wales. Edward was invested in Wales in 1301, and the tradition has continued ever since. In 1969, Prince Charles was invested as the current Prince of Wales in Caernarfon's courtyard, watched by a worldwide television audience of millions.

The great creamy-grey walls of Edward I's castle dominate the little market town of Caernarfon. Building started in 1283, but a decade later the unfinished fortress came under attack during a Welsh rebellion, and considerable damage was done. Believing he could not trust the native Welsh, Edward press-ganged English craftsmen and labourers to rebuild the castle, creating what still remains the grandest and most impressive of all Welsh castles. Edward intended his castle to be not only a fortress, but also the seat of his government in Wales and his own official residence there. The massive building was also a clear statement of English victory over a defeated nation.

Caernarfon Castle is shaped like an hourglass. Great walls with stones in banded colours (inspired by the walls of Constantinople, which Edward admired while on a crusade) run between the great towers, topped by battlemented wall-walks. The defences of the castle were formidable. In order to gain access to the courtyard, visitors were obliged to cross two drawbridges, pass through five heavy doors and walk under six portcullises. The entire way was protected by a range of arrow slits and murder holes, through which an unpleasant array of deadly missiles could be hurled down onto unwelcome guests.

Each of the towers is different. The Eagle Tower, named for the majestic carved eagles that once adorned the turrets, had a water gate, so that supplies could be brought in by sea in the event of the castle being besieged by land. The Queen's Tower contained spacious living apartments, and today houses the Royal Welch Fusiliers Museum. The Queen's Gate was also intended to provide some lavish accommodation, but it was never completed.

Caernarfon was the most ambitious of Edward's great castles in Wales and it was just one of 17 that Edward built, remodelled or ordered his barons to construct between 1276 and 1296.

CAERPHILLY CASTLE Caerphilly

8 miles (13km) north of Cardiff | Open daily all year | Tel: 029 2088 3143 | www.cadw.wales.gov.uk

When the huge water systems that make up some of the defences of Caerphilly Castle are taken into account, this is one of the biggest, and certainly one of the most spectacular, military complexes in Britain. The sheer size of the defences at Caerphilly can truly be appreciated only from a distance, taking in the vast outer walls, the lakes and the inner concentric castle itself.

After 1066, the Normans established themselves in southern Wales, although they left the unfarmable land in the north to the Welsh. In the mid-13th century, the last of the Welsh-born princes, Llywelyn the Last, decided that he should unite Wales under his own rule. He began to threaten the lands held by the Normans, causing Henry III to build a number of castles to protect them. One such castle was Caerphilly, on which work started in 1268, funded by the wealthy baron Gilbert de Clare, Earl of Gloucester and Hertford. Two years later, Llywelyn attacked. How much damage was actually done to the fledgling castle is not known, but de Clare ordered that building should be completed as soon as possible. When Llywelyn attacked again in 1271 he was repelled, and although he was said to have claimed he could have taken it in three days, Caerphilly's defences were probably sufficiently developed to render this an idle boast.

The castle itself comprises a rectangular enclosure with outer and inner walls. The inner walls contain two great gatehouses and the remains of the Great Hall. Here, in the heart of the castle, the living quarters were situated, along with domestic buildings such as kitchens, storerooms, a chapel, butteries and pantries. The outer walls, well fortified with towers and their own gatehouses, gave additional protection to the inner ward and were surrounded by a moat. Beyond the moat, to the east, lay a further complex of defences in the form of great walls studded with towers. The artificial lake lent protection to the north and south sides, while the west was defended by a walled island.

After the death of de Clare's son, Caerphilly passed to Hugh Despenser, the favourite of Edward II. Edward himself took refuge here from his estranged wife and her lover, although he was forced to flee when she besieged the castle, leaving behind half his treasure and most of his clothes.

Oliver Cromwell ordered Caerphilly to be slighted during the English Civil War. After the Civil War was over, local people stole Caerphilly's stones to build houses, and subsidence caused one of its towers to lean dramatically to one side.

Caerphilly Castle, viewed from Castle Street (left) and across the huge defensive artificial lake (below)

CARDIFF CASTLE Cardiff

Cardiff city centre | Open daily all year | Tel: 029 2087 8100 | www.cardiffcastle.com

The site of Cardiff Castle was known to the Romans, who built a fortress here. When the Normans arrived in the 11th century, they built a motte about 40 feet (12m) high, and topped it with a wooden building. Later, a 12-sided keep was erected, and a gatehouse and stairs were added in the 15th century. Robert, the eldest son of William the Conqueror, was held prisoner here for many years by his youngest brother, Henry I, and died in Cardiff Castle in 1134.

A short distance away from the keep on the hill is a magnificent Victorian reconstruction. These buildings owe their existence to the rich 3rd Marquess of Bute. Bute had long been fascinated by history and employed William Burges, an architect who shared his love of the past, to construct a great palace in the style of a medieval castle. Burges designed rooms with intricately painted ceilings, elaborately marbled bathrooms, spiral staircases and an impressive clock tower. The Banqueting Hall is the largest room in the castle, and has a fine wooden roof, liberally decorated with brightly coloured shields. The high walls have murals showing scenes from the Civil War, as well as a small painting of the Conqueror's son, Robert, gazing wistfully from behind his barred prison window.

There are guided tours, a Firing Line exhibition (which tells the history of the Welsh soldier over the last 300 years) and fabulous banquets available all year. Booking is essential for the banquets.

Fine carving in the Banqueting Hall (right and far right) inside magnificent Cardiff Castle (below)

ROBERTVS CONSVL COM GLŌ

CAREW CASTLE Pembrokeshire

5 miles (8km) east of Pembroke | Open daily all year | Tel: 01646 651782 | **www.carewcastle.com**

Although today Carew appears to be more of a palace than a castle, it still possesses some of its original defensive features. Of these, perhaps the most impressive are the

two great cylindrical towers with their jutting bases. Parts of the medieval castle were altered in the 15th and 16th centuries, when its many different owners built new wings and exchanged the small, narrow windows for larger, stately ones.

One of Carew's first owners is said to have been Gerald of Windsor, who was married to a Welsh princess named Nest. Before her marriage, Nest had been a hostage of Henry I, and legend has it that she bore his illegitimate son. Nest's grandson was Gerald of Wales, whose detailed description of life in the 12th century is an important source of information for medieval historians.

Another legend attached to Carew is that of Sir Roland Rhys, who lived in the

castle during the reign of James I. When his son eloped with the daughter of a Flemish merchant, Rhys attacked the merchant with the help of his pet ape. Later, the ape attacked Rhys himself, and during the struggle that followed, the castle caught fire. However, the most serious damage to be inflicted on Carew's elegant buildings occurred during the ferocious battles of the English Civil War in the 17th century.

Within the delightful grounds of Carew Castle there is an interesting old restored tidal mill, which is open to visitors from April to the end of October.

Carew Castle is located on the coast within the beautiful Pembrokeshire Coast National Park

CASTELL COCH Cardiff

6 miles (10km) north west of Cardiff, in Tongwynlais | Open daily all year | Tel: 029 2081 0101 | www.cadw.wales.gov.uk

Rising out of wooded parklands, and clearly visible from the main road from Cardiff to Pontypridd, stands Castell Coch, a vast, elegant building with conical towers and a working drawbridge. Castell Coch, meaning 'red castle' in Welsh (it is built of red sandstone), is just like a castle from some fairytale. It was built during the 19th century, at a time when Victorians were expressing a great interest in the past, especially in the seemingly idyllic, industry-free Middle Ages.

Castell Coch was designed by the architect William Burges for the 3rd Marquess of Bute, and it was not the first time these two men had worked together. They were also responsible for work on Cardiff Castle, with Bute providing the fortune and Burges the plans. Castell Coch was never intended to be a permanent residence, but was, in Burges' words, 'for occasional occupation in the summer'. It even has a dungeon, but the only prisoners have been actors, since Castell Coch has proved to be a popular, ready-made film set.

If the romantic exterior of the castle is impressive, the interior is a breathtaking jumble of rich colours and minute attention to detail. There are fabulously decorated ceilings in many rooms, while others boast intricately painted wall panels. The total effect is the kind of exuberant gaudiness that is indisputably Victorian.

Below and right: A fairytale castle set amidst woods

Below right: Castell Coch's Octagonal Room is a mix of rich colours and fabulous detail

71

CASTELL-Y-BERE Gwynedd

9 miles (14.5km) south of Dolgellau | Open access all year | www.cadw.wales.gov.uk

This once-powerful Welsh-built castle is dwarfed by the mountains that tower over it. Cader Idris is one of the great peaks looming steeply over the site of Castell-y-Bere. The castle is reached by a path that leads around the rocky spur on which it is perched, and approaching from this angle gives an accurate impression of the natural strength of the site. Castell-y-Bere once controlled one of the primary routes through central Wales, but today the major road runs further south

and the castle is abandoned and lonely. Little remains, and most of the buildings are represented by foundations alone.

It was originally built by Llywelyn the Great in the 1220s, probably more as a step towards securing his own position as Prince of Wales in the minds of his warring compatriots than to stand against the invading Normans. The castle was roughly triangular, following the shape of the rock, with towers at each angle. The entrance was

defended by an impressive array of ditches, as well as a drawbridge and a portcullis.

During Edward I's wars against the Welsh princes, Castell-y-Bere was besieged and damaged. Although Edward paid more than £260 to have the castle repaired, it was not occupied for long, and was completely abandoned by about 1295.

A shaft of evening sunlight illuminates the ruins of Castell-y-Bere near Tal-y-Llyn in Snowdonia

CHEPSTOW CASTLE Monmouthshire

15 miles (24km) east of Newport | Open daily all year | Tel: 01291 624065 | www.cadw.wales.gov.uk

Chepstow was one of the first stone castles ever to be built in Britain. It was started in 1068, a mere two years after the invasion of England by William the Conqueror. William knew that in order to continue to hold what he had acquired at the Battle of Hastings, it was necessary to dominate the newly conquered people with a show of Norman power. This was achieved by a spate of castle building – at first simple mounds topped with wooden structures, and later more permanent stone towers.

Chepstow was of great strategic importance, and William entrusted one of his best generals, William FitzOsbern, to build the castle and control the Marches. FitzOsbern chose a site that was naturally protected on one side by cliffs plummeting down into the brown waters of the Wye, and on another by a valley. He protected the remaining sides with stone walls. The very first building was a simple, two-storeyed rectangular keep with some fine arched windows.

In around 1190, Chepstow Castle passed to the Marshall family, who then set about improving its defences by adding strong curtain walls with towers set into them. They extended the castle too, and these alterations divided the castle into four separate sections, each leading into the other from east to west. The Marshalls were also responsible for the imposing gatehouse that looms over present-day visitors as they enter the castle. The gatehouse has a prison in one of its round towers, a dismal chamber with only an airshaft to break the monotony of the dank walls.

After 1270 a second hall, a D-shaped tower and another gatehouse were built on to the castle by one of Edward I's most powerful barons, Roger Bigod. Bigod's buildings contained comfortable living quarters, with well-equipped kitchens, larders and storerooms. A double-seated latrine was also provided for visitors to the hall, and its waste was discharged down the steep cliffs above the river.

Although Chepstow was never besieged in medieval times, it played an important role in the Civil War, coming under siege twice while it was being held for King Charles I. The garrison surrendered the first time, but fell after a fierce battle on the second occasion. Marten's Tower is named after Henry Marten, one of the Cromwellians who signed Charles I's death warrant. Marten was held prisoner here after the monarchy had been restored.

After the Civil War, the importance of Chepstow Castle gradually declined and it began to fall into the romantic ruin it is today.

Ancient stone steps lead down to the cellar (left) in the ruins of Chepstow Castle (above)

CONWY CASTLE Conwy

Eight massive round towers and two barbicans linked by thick walls form the castle at Conwy, which, although perhaps overshadowed by Caernarfon, is one of the most spectacular in Wales.

Building at Conwy began in 1283 and was completed around 1287. During this very short time, the town's defences were also built, taking in some ¾ mile (1.2km) of walls with 22 towers and three gateways. Conwy was Edward I's most expensive Welsh castle and was designed by his talented castle architect Master James of St George. Although Conwy's eight circular towers are its most dominant feature, there are the remains of other buildings in the two wards. One is the huge Great Hall, which would have been the heart of the medieval castle, where meals were eaten communally and audiences held, and where some people would have slept.

Shortly after Conwy was built, there was a Welsh rebellion led by Prince Madog, in which a number of Edward I's castles were badly damaged. Edward marched to Wales in order to suppress the rebellion, setting up his headquarters at Conwy. However, as soon as he was inside the castle, the river flooded, trapping Edward and his men inside. They were stranded for several days, and supplies of food and fresh water became dangerously low before the waters receded and they were able to escape.

Telford's suspension bridge (right and below) leads to Conwy Castle, spectacularly floodlit at night (far right)

CRICCIETH CASTLE Gwynedd

5 miles (8km) west of Porthmadog | Open daily Apr to end Oct, Fri to Sun in winter | Tel: 01766 522227 | www.cadw.wales.gov.uk

In 1404 Criccieth Castle was taken from the English by Owain Glyndwr, the last of the Welsh leaders to rebel against the English crown. Shortly afterwards, the castle was so badly damaged by fire that it was never used again. In the 1930s, an archaeological investigation found proof of the fire that brought the castle's role in history to such an abrupt end, when charred timbers dating from the 15th century were discovered.

Criccieth, like many castles, was built in several different stages. The first stage, which included the solid twin-towered gatehouse, was built by Llywelyn the Great, while his grandson, Llywelyn the Last, added more walls and a rectangular tower. Edward I took the castle after Llywelyn the Last's defeat, and ordered the building of more walls and a tower strong enough to mount a siege engine on the roof.

Today, Criccieth is in ruins, although its commanding position on a promontory overlooking the picturesque Tremadog Bay gives an idea of the status this castle must once have enjoyed. Llywelyn the Great's massive gatehouse still presents a forbidding face to the world, and the thickness of its crumbling walls still imbues it with an aura of strength and permanence.

DENBIGH CASTLE Denbighshire

9 miles (14km) north west of Ruthin | Open daily Apr to end Oct (open but unstaffed in winter) | Tel: 01745 813385 | www.cadw.wales.gov.uk

Standing among the crumbling walls of Denbigh Castle, it is not difficult to imagine the former splendour and power of this now-ruined castle. It sits on top of a hill overlooking the town, commanding fine views of the surrounding countryside, and even in decay still exudes a feeling of Norman dominance.

Denbigh's most impressive feature is its great gatehouse, although the centuries have not treated it kindly. It was almost triangular, and was made up of three interlinked octagonal towers. The front part has an elegant arched door, while the stonework around it is of an unusual chequered pattern made up of different coloured stones. Above the door there is a niche that still holds a statue of Edward I, now very weathered.

Because Edward I's funds for castle building were not unlimited, he persuaded as many of his barons as he could to build castles for him. Denbigh was such a castle, and was built between 1282 and 1311 by Henry de Lacey, Earl of Lincoln. An unusual feature is the steeply sloping barbican that protected the back of the castle.

Denbigh's most famous son, Henry Morton Stanley (1841–1904), the journalist-turned-explorer, spent his early years living in a cottage in the castle grounds.

Crumbling walls are all that is left of Denbigh Castle

DOLBADARN CASTLE Gwynedd

7½ miles (12km) east of Caernarfon | Open access all year | www.cadw.wales.gov.uk

Huge, steep-sided mountains loom on both sides of the Llanberis Pass as the road winds down towards Caernarfon and the coast. Here can be found Dolbadarn Castle, still standing sentinel to the route it once guarded. Although Dolbadarn was never large, it was of great importance to the Welsh princes. When Llywelyn the Last retreated to his mountain stronghold to escape from Edward I, the Llanberis Pass was the main route to the farmlands of Anglesey, from where most of Llywelyn's supplies came.

The castle's most striking feature is the single round tower that still survives to a height of 40 feet (12m). The entry was on the first floor, via a flight of wooden steps that could be pulled up inside the castle in the event of an attack. The tower was probably built by Llywelyn the Great in the early 13th century, and is much stronger and better built than the rest of the castle, of which little remains but the foundations. On one side of the castle lie gently undulating hills with the lake twinkling in the distance, while on the other stand the stark mountains of Snowdonia National Park, some ripped open by slate quarries.

One of the most remarkable aspects of Dolbadarn Castle (right) is the lake and mountain view (above)

DOLWYDDELAN CASTLE Gwynedd

6 miles (10km) south west of Betws-y-Coed | Open daily all year | Tel: 01690 750366 | www.cadw.wales.gov.uk

This sturdy three-storeyed tower appears almost insignificant among the sweeping hills of the Welsh countryside, especially next to the rugged green-brown slopes of Moel-Siabod that lie to one side. The precise origins of the castle are obscured by time, but it was built by the princes of Wales to guard the ancient pathway that ran from Meirionnydd to the Vale of Conwy. It may have been built by Lorwerth Drwyndwn (meaning 'the flat nosed' or 'broken nosed'), and it is said that one of Wales' most famous princes, Llywelyn the Great, was born here around 1173.

Edward I's forces attacked Dolwyddelan Castle in 1283 during his Welsh campaign, and seeing its great strategic value, the King had it refortified and manned by English soldiers; thus the Welsh-built castle became a stronghold for the English. The castle itself was originally a rectangular tower of two storeys; it was later given an extra floor and a battlemented roof line. Later still, thick walls were added to form an enclosure with another rectangular tower, all protected by ditches cut into the rock. Although it was built by the Welsh, the architect of Dolwyddelan had borrowed heavily from the Norman style of castle building. There was an entrance on the first floor, protected from intruders by a drawbridge.

Dolwyddelan Castle is set in the ruggedly beautiful countryside of Snowdonia National Park

FLINT CASTLE Flintshire

10 miles (16km) north west of Chester | Open access all year | www.cadw.wales.gov.uk

In August 1399 King Richard II, fleeing from the forces of his cousin Henry of Bolingbroke, arrived at Flint Castle. Within days, Bolingbroke (known as the Usurper King) had captured Richard and had him taken to London, where he was forced to abdicate in Bolingbroke's favour. Bolingbroke then declared himself King Henry IV, and Richard was eventually taken to Pontefract Castle in Yorkshire, where he was probably murdered.

Flint was the first of the castles built by Edward I during his Welsh campaigns. Building started in 1277 with an enormous workforce of 2,300 labourers, who were paid handsomely, since building a castle in a hostile land was hard and dangerous work. The castle consisted of a rectangular enclosure with four round towers at the corners. This was further protected by additional walls, a moat and some deep ditches. One of the round corner towers was larger than the others, and was protected by its own moat. It also had its own kitchens, living quarters and chapel, and was probably the residence of the constable and his family.

Nowadays, this once vitally important castle is hidden behind the modern town, bypassed by tourists heading west and standing lonely and forgotten on the marshy shores of the River Dee.

Flint Castle's most impressive feature is a solitary round tower (above), isolated from the rest (below)

GROSMONT CASTLE Monmouthshire

12 miles (19km) north west of Monmouth | Open access all year | www.cadw.wales.gov.uk

Three castles – Grosmont, Skenfrith and White – were built by the Normans to protect this important sector of the Marches. At first, the castles were only wooden structures strengthened by earthworks. But continued Welsh rebellion against Norman rule meant that more permanent fortresses were needed, and one of King John's barons, Hubert de Burgh, Earl of Kent, set out to provide them. However, the favour of medieval kings was an uncertain thing to hold, and Hubert lost his 'Three Castles' twice during his chequered career.

Thus the Three Castles had at least two main building phases. Hubert started the first stone building at Grosmont in 1201,

mainly comprising the rectangular hall. When Hubert held the Three Castles for the second time, between 1219 and 1232, he added a gatehouse and the round towers.

Grosmont Castle has certainly seen some action during its 800-year history. It was attacked by the Welsh in 1233, and Owain Glyndwr laid siege to it in 1405. Grosmont is also associated with Jack O'Kent, a local folk hero. The devil vowed to take O'Kent, whether he was buried in the church or outside it. For that reason, O'Kent arranged to be buried under the wall of the village church, so that he is neither inside nor out.

Right and below: The haunting ruins of Grosmont Castle

HARLECH CASTLE Gwynedd

16 miles (26km) south of Porthmadog | Open daily all year | Tel: 01766 780552 | www.cadw.wales.gov.uk

The last great uprising of the Welsh against the occupying English occurred in the early 15th century under the leadership of Welsh hero Owain Glyndwr. In the spring of 1404, Glyndwr gathered his forces against the mighty fortress of Harlech, but the castle was too strong to be taken in a battle and so Glyndwr began a siege. For many months the castle garrison held out, despite Glyndwr's efficient blockade of all the castle's supply routes. Food ran low, then disease broke out, doubtless aggravated by the shortage of clean water for drinking, cooking and washing. After some soldiers made an unsuccessful escape bid, Glyndwr stood at the castle's gate and demanded surrender.

Harlech was Glyndwr's home and headquarters for the next four years, and it is possible he even held a Welsh parliament here. It is also said that he crowned himself Prince of Wales at Harlech. Finally, in 1409, Henry IV sent a powerful force to recapture the castle and stamp out the rebellion. After a short siege, the castle fell. Glyndwr's wife and children were taken prisoner, and although Glyndwr himself escaped, the fall of Harlech marked the beginning of the end for him. Within four years he had disappeared.

The great castle that allowed its garrison to withstand intense and prolonged sieges was one of Edward I's 'iron ring' of castles built during his second castle-building campaign. Unlike Beaumaris, on which building continued for 35 years, Harlech was completed within seven years (1283–90). Master builder James of St George (1230–1308) personally supervised the building, and it does not take much imagination to envisage what a remarkable feat of engineering was required to erect such a vast fortress in such a short space of time.

Harlech is a concentric castle, with outer walls designed to provide a layer of further protection for the vulnerable inner walls, which contained the main living quarters. The inner walls also contain the great gatehouse, with its comfortable residential apartments. The gatehouse is perhaps Harlech's finest feature – a vast structure that presents a forbidding display of thick grey walls and impregnability.

Harlech's mighty castle walls were not its only defence. Two sides were protected by deep dry moats hacked out of the rock on which the castle stands, while near-vertical cliffs plunged down to the sea, making an assault on the back of the castle virtually impossible. However, there was a gated and fortified stairway (known as the 'Way of the Sea') leading from the castle down to the sea, which meant that the castle could be supplied by ships if the land was blockaded. The tide level receded in the 19th century, and today the sea is about half a mile away from the castle.

Previous page, below and right: Views of magnificent Harlech Castle, including a 19th-century etching

Below: Kidwelly Castle's imposing gatehouse

Right: Spiral staircase leading down to Constable's Hall

Below right: Kidwelly church seen from the castle

The early history of this well-preserved castle was tempestuous. It was Roger, the Bishop of Salisbury, who first put up earthworks on the site, some of which can still be seen in the semicircular ditch that curves around the present castle. In 1231, Llywelyn the Great attacked the Norman castle, causing considerable damage. Its owner at that time, Patrick de Chaworth, rebuilt the castle and it withstood another attack in the 1250s. Most of the building that remains today, however, dates from the 1270s.

The main castle forms a rectangle, with great circular towers at each corner. A semicircular wall sweeps around one side and the site is protected by defensive earthworks. Unusually, the great gatehouse is not a part of the inner walls, as in other castles, but rather forms part of the outer walls. The most likely reason for this is that there was not enough firm ground inside the castle to support such a large building.

The many small rooms and chambers in the walls and towers of Kidwelly, and the narrow interconnecting passages and stairs, give a particularly vivid sense of what life must have been like in a medieval castle.

LAUGHARNE CASTLE Carmarthenshire

14 miles (22km) south west of Carmarthen | Open daily Apr to end Oct | Tel: 01994 427906 | www.cadw.wales.gov.uk

The Laugharne Castle that can be seen today bears very little resemblance to the building that was erected in the 12th century. This original castle was seized from the English by Welsh princes three times before the end of the 13th century: by Rhys ap Gruffydd, Llywelyn the Great, and Llywelyn the Last. Parts of the ivy-clad building that can be visited today date from the early 14th century, and the gatehouse is thought to be 15th century. The grand entrance arch in the gateway was added later still, probably during the 16th century.

In Tudor times, Laugharne was leased to Sir John Perrott, said to be the illegitimate son of Henry VIII, who did not find the medieval castle to his courtly taste and set about converting it into a fine Tudor mansion. The foundations of his hall can be seen in the courtyard near the well.

Laugharne Castle came under siege during the Civil War, and some of the cannonballs fired at it by the Roundheads have been found deeply embedded in its sturdy stone battlements.

The small town of Laugharne is perhaps best known for being the home of the great Welsh poet Dylan Thomas (1914–53).

Laugharne Castle was familiar to Dylan Thomas, who wrote in The Boathouse, on its outer walls (below right)

88

LLANSTEFFAN CASTLE Carmarthenshire

8 miles (13km) south west of Carmarthen | Open access all year | www.cadw.wales.gov.uk

Running like a finger across the gently undulating farmland of the coast is a ridge that ends in a rocky bluff. The advantages of this site for defence were recognized long before the Normans arrived, and charcoal from an Iron Age hill fort has been dated to the 6th century BC.

When the Normans established themselves in Wales, they were quick to make use of this ready-made site, protected on three sides by natural slopes, and a ditch was dug to strengthen the fourth side. The castle has two baileys, or enclosed areas. The smaller area is the older of the two, and the small square tower, which can still be seen, was defended by battlemented walls.

When the Welsh took Llansteffan in 1257 (with embarrassing ease), the English de Camville family decided it was time to make improvements to the castle's defences. They built thick protective outer walls around the lower bailey, as well as several towers and a fine gatehouse. In Tudor times the gatehouse was converted from a functional military building into a comfortable residence. Before Llansteffan came into the hands of Cadw to be carefully restored as an historic monument, it was used as farm buildings for some 400 years.

Medieval Llansteffan Castle, by day (right) and at dusk (below), seen from the Tywi estuary

LUDLOW CASTLE Shropshire

12 miles (19km) north of Leominster | Open most days all year | Tel: 01584 874465 | www.ludlowcastle.com

Throughout 1138, England was wracked by a civil war fought between supporters of King Stephen and his cousin Empress Matilda, both of whom believed they were the rightful heir to the English throne. Stephen laid siege to the castle at Ludlow, which was then held by one of Matilda's supporters. While Stephen was walking outside the castle walls with Prince Henry of Scotland, a metal hook on a rope was lowered from the castle, catching on Prince Henry's cloak. As the terrified

Prince began to rise up the walls, quick-thinking Stephen cut the rope and managed to free him. He did not, however, take the castle, and was forced to abandon his siege and fight elsewhere.

The extensive ruins of Ludlow Castle contain much that is interesting or unusual. There is a circular chapel, which is modelled on the Church of the Holy Sepulchre in Jerusalem and is one of only six round churches in England. There are curtain walls

with flanking towers that are among the earliest such defensive features in England, and a gatehouse that was later blocked up to make a square tower and then, later still, reduced in size. Many of the existing domestic buildings, such as the kitchens, halls and service rooms, were built in the 14th century but were given Tudor facelifts.

Glorious Ludlow Castle was described as 'the very perfection of decay' by author Daniel Defoe

90

MANORBIER CASTLE Pembrokeshire

The strong limestone walls of Manorbier Castle have weathered the centuries well and still stand largely intact after 800 years. The first stone buildings were a three-storeyed square tower and a long hall. In the 13th century the curtain walls were raised, with flanking towers and a fine gatehouse. Two large barns were built in the castle in the 17th century.

Manorbier's considerable defences, including the sturdy walls, battlements, portcullises and ditches, were never put to the test by a serious siege, and the Norman de Barri family lived their lives unassailed by attacks from the local Welsh people.

Left: The church with its limewash-painted white tower, seen from a castle window

Below and right: The castle is situated amid the breathtaking scenery of the Pembrokeshire coast

Manorbier Castle is perhaps most famous as the birthplace of Giraldus Cambrensis, or Gerald of Wales as he is also known. Gerald was a highly respected scholar who travelled extensively before he became an archdeacon, and his sensitive and incisive observations (written in high-quality Latin) provide an extremely valuable record of life in medieval Wales and Ireland.

Beside his analyses of Welsh politics and history, he described the people and their way of life – how they slept on communal beds of rushes wearing all their clothes, and how their feuding and vengeful natures were balanced by their love of music and poetry.

PEMBROKE CASTLE Pembrokeshire

Pembroke Castle's most outstanding feature is its great tower – a vast circular keep that stands almost 80 feet (24m) high, with walls that are 16½ feet (5m) at the thickest part, all capped by an unusual stone dome. Although the keep once had four floors, these have long since disappeared, and today you can stand in the basement and gaze all the way up to the stone dome itself. The great tower was built between 1200 and 1210, probably by William Marshall, one of Richard I's most powerful barons. William Marshall (c. 1146–1219) once defeated Richard the Lionheart in a fight and could have killed him. Years later, Richard remembered Marshall's act of mercy and made him the Earl of Pembroke.

There are two other unusual features to notice about this castle. The first is the wonderful medieval graffiti scored into the plaster walls of the Monkton Tower, and the second is the 'Wogan', a great natural cavern under the castle that can be reached by a spiral staircase.

The castle – with its great battlemented walls liberally studded with defensive towers and a mighty gatehouse – was besieged by Cromwell during the Civil War. Once the defending garrison had surrendered, Cromwell blew up the barbican and some of the towers to ensure that Pembroke Castle could not become a refuge for Royalist forces again. Much of the castle was restored during the last century.

All kinds of fascinating events take place throughout the year at the castle, including falconry displays, battle re-enactments, craft shows and theatrical performances. Shakespeare's plays are regularly performed here, with the castle environs providing a fitting historical backdrop to the bard's most popular works.

Battle re-enactments (right) and other special events take place regularly at Pembroke Castle (above)

Built in 1820–35 from pink sandstone, this part of the
castle (above) includes the staff quarters and stables

The Grand Staircase (overleaf), designed by Thomas
Hopper, was built in 1820–37 in neo-Norman style

This vast 19th-century neo-Norman castle is situated in some of Wales' most picturesque countryside. Building a vast Victorian mansion in the style of a Norman castle is not unheard of, but what makes Penrhyn Castle so unusual is that, whereas most structures are simply a facade concealing a comfortable range of family rooms, here the theme continues throughout the interior. The castle was built between 1820 and 1845 on the site of a medieval, fortified manor house – and a spiral staircase from the original structure can still be seen.

Thomas Hopper was the bold architect who created this imaginatively forbidding fantasy structure for George Dawkins Pennant, a local slate-quarry owner, whose family made their fortune from Welsh slate and Jamaican sugar.

Hopper's commission also included the suitable fitting out of the interiors of the castle with panelling, plasterwork and furniture. Most of the furniture is 19th-century 'Norman', and includes a slate bed weighing over a ton (made for Queen Victoria when she visited in 1859), and a brass bed made especially for Edward VII at the then enormous cost of £600.

The most notable of the rooms include the Great Hall, which is heated by the Roman hypocaust method of underfloor hot air, the wonderful library with its heavily decorated ceiling and the dining room, covered with neo-Norman decoration. The grand staircase is quite startling in both its proportions – three full storeys high – and its cathedral-like structure of lofty arches, carved stonework and stained glass.

There is an industrial railway museum in the courtyard, a model railway museum and a doll museum; and the whole ensemble is set in 40 acres (16ha) of beautiful grounds between Snowdonia and the Menai Strait, overlooking the North Wales coast.

Right: The heart of the home: the kitchen at Penrhyn Castle is fitted with a gas stove under the arch-shaped windows. A variety of copper pans and a large kettle give an idea of the scale of the catering operation required when the castle was fully occupied

RAGLAN CASTLE Monmouthshire

7 miles (11km) south west of Monmouth | Open daily all year | Tel: 01291 690228 | www.cadw.wales.gov.uk

It is said that Charles I played bowls on the grass on Raglan's terraces, under the shadow of the great Yellow Tower of Gwent, the most imposing part of this magnificent 15th-century castle. The story goes that the local bowls champion was called upon to provide an able competitor, and horrified the King's class-conscious entourage by proudly pointing out his house in the village.

A short time later, the country was at war, and Charles relied on more from Raglan and his Welsh subjects than a good game of bowls. At that time, Raglan was owned by the Earl of Worcester, who immediately garrisoned the castle for the King. Cromwellian forces laid siege to the castle in June 1646, and the powerful walls underwent weeks of devastating bombardment. On 19 August Worcester was forced to surrender,

The Yellow Tower at Raglan Castle (below) and the entire site, viewed from a hot-air balloon (right)

and Cromwell's troops poured into the castle. Worcester was taken to London, where he soon died, and Raglan Castle was stripped of anything portable and left derelict. Further destruction took place after the Restoration, when the newly created Duke of Beaufort ransacked Raglan for fittings for his new home at Badminton. By the 19th century Raglan was a romantic, ivy-clad ruin.

There had been a castle at Raglan since about 1070, and there are records to suggest that the original castle survived until well into the early 1400s. This building fell into the hands of William ap Thomas, a Welsh knight who had fought at the Battle of Agincourt with Henry V. Thomas began to build a tower in an unusual hexagonal shape, a four-storeyed keep with thick, tapering walls.

He surrounded the tower with more walls and a moat, and the pale gold stone from which it is built earned it its name: the Yellow Tower of Gwent. Thomas's son William, Earl of Pembroke, continued the building work, and added the Pitched Stone Court and the Great Gatehouse. He also rebuilt much of the Fountain Court, and made it into gracious living quarters for his family. William, a Yorkist, was defeated at the Battle of Edgecote, and was executed by Warwick, 'The Kingmaker'.

Standing between Raglan's two courtyards is the Great Hall, mainly Elizabethan in origin. Worcester entertained on a lavish scale here, and it is easy to imagine these grand occasions with his guests sitting at long tables, and the fine stained glass casting patterned light into the room.

RHUDDLAN CASTLE Denbighshire

🦁 **3 miles (5km) south of Rhyl | Open daily Apr to end Oct | Tel: 01745 590777 | www.cadw.wales.gov.uk**

This concentric castle built by Edward I now stands uncomfortably next to a modern housing development. Its once-powerful round towers are crumbling; time has eaten away at their roofless tops. Yet Rhuddlan was a vital part of Edward I's campaign in Wales and was designed by master castle-builder James of St George. Indeed, it was here that the Great Statute of Wales was issued in March 1284, proclaiming Edward's dominance over the defeated country.

Rhuddlan Castle is diamond-shaped with towers at each corner, and has two sets of outer walls. It also has its own dock tower. The building of the castle in its present location necessitated a great feat of military engineering. The site was already historically important because it was on a ford over the River Clwyd. Edward wanted his new castle to have access to the sea, so that it might be supplied by boats, but the Clwyd was a shallow river that meandered lazily towards the sea. Edward cut a new channel, deeper and straighter than the natural one, and 700 years later it still follows this course.

Rhuddlan Castle by the River Clwyd, designed by Master James of St George for King Edward I

TRETOWER CASTLE Powys

There was a Norman castle on this site as early as 1100, consisting of a mound with a wooden structure perched on top. This wooden castle was converted to a stone building in the 12th century, and thick walls were added. At this point it was discovered that the castle's water supply was seeping below the mound and undermining it, and so additional stone foundations had to be laid to prevent subsidence.

In the early 13th century, this castle was pulled down and a circular tower built in its place. It had walls that were nine feet (2.7m) thick, and the bottom splayed outwards to make it more difficult to undermine. This stalwart round tower, with its small Norman arched windows, still stands among the trees of the beautiful Usk Valley.

The workmanship of the wooden-ceilinged hall is a much admired feature of Tretower Castle

In the early 15th century, Tretower Court was rebuilt on the site of an earlier house by its owner, Sir Robert Vaughan. The Court, with its magnificent wooden-ceilinged hall, remained the home of the Vaughan family until 1783. The buildings are still fairly well preserved, although some parts have been reconstructed. The sliding shutters in the gallery and the elegant wood-panelled partition are of particular interest. There is also a recreated 15th-century garden within the castle grounds.

WHITE CASTLE Monmouthshire

7 miles (11km) north east of Abergavenny | Open daily Apr to end Oct (open but unstaffed in winter) | Tel: 01600 780380 | www.cadw.wales.gov.uk

White Castle gained its name from the white plaster that once covered it, but only traces of this can be seen today on the castle's crumbling walls. White's sister castles, Grosmont and Skenfrith, were built by Hubert de Burgh. While he owned the so-called Three Castles of Gwent between 1201 and 1204 and from 1219 to 1232, White itself had a rather different origin.

Like Skenfrith and Grosmont, White Castle began as earthworks with wooden buildings. In the 12th century, a stone curtain wall was added, and in the 13th century a gatehouse and additional towers were built. White Castle was near to land claimed by Welsh prince Llywelyn the Last during his wars with Edward I, and the King ensured that its defences were strengthened. Even in its ruined state, the complexity and sophistication of the castle's defences can be appreciated, especially the height and strength of the great walls.

In 1941, Rudolf Hess, Adolf Hitler's second in command, flew to Scotland to try to negotiate a peace treaty with Great Britain. Treated as a prisoner of war, he was moved to Wales and held for a while at a hospital near White Castle, and was taken sometimes to feed the swans in the castle moat.

A footbridge leads to the inner ward of White Castle, where some of the stonework dates from 1184

6

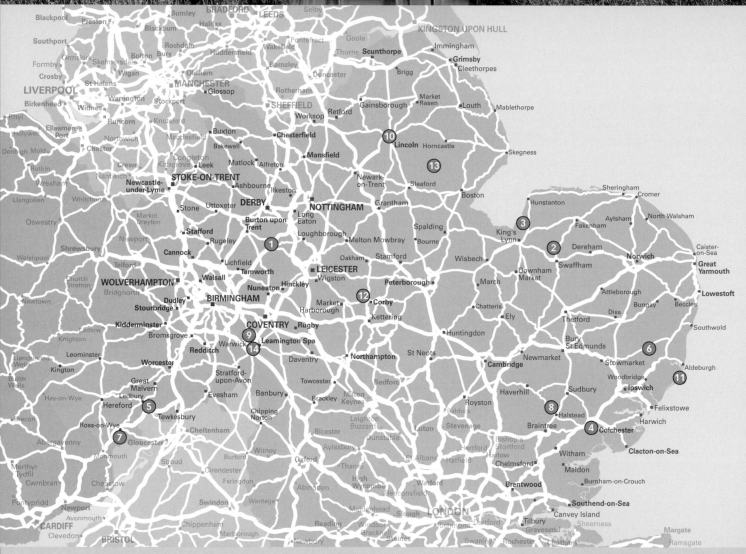

CENTRAL ENGLAND & EAST ANGLIA | 4

Evidence of its important place in history can be seen all around this region, as much of its rural landscape, character and traditions have been preserved. The Romans stayed for 400 years and were the first to drain the Fens. They made Colchester the capital of Britain, and Colchester Castle was built on the foundations of the Roman temple of Claudius, from stones taken from nearby Roman ruins. Mighty Kenilworth Castle, with its deep red stone, was the scene of one of Britain's most important sieges, lasting for more than six months. Framlingham Castle was used by Queen Elizabeth I as a prison for priests who defied the new Church of England.

Because of its geographical position, the central area of England was continually crossed by armies, from Edward I's conquest of Wales in 1282–83, to the Wars of the Roses in 1455–87. Due to its more out-of-the-way situation, East Anglia has been somewhat less ravaged by marching boots over the centuries. One of eastern England's best-known castles is Castle Rising, famous for its connection with Edward II's Queen Isabella, who spent the last 30 years of her life there.

ASHBY DE LA ZOUCH CASTLE Leicestershire

9 miles (14km) south east of Burton upon Trent | Open daily Apr to Oct and selected days in winter | Tel: 01530 413343 | www.english-heritage.org.uk

A hall was founded at Ashby in the 12th century, but its principal feature, the keep, was not built until the 15th century. The owner, William, Lord Hastings, was granted a licence to convert the hall into a castle in 1474, at the same time as he started building his picturesque fortified house at Kirby Muxloe. Hastings' keep was about 90 feet (27m) tall and had four floors. There was also an extension on the north east side of the tower, which had seven floors. Although there were already two wells in the castle, the keep had another of its own – a sensible precaution, for it meant that no one could tamper with the water supply.

Lord Hastings' own story shows how fortunes and the favour of kings could rise and fall in the Middle Ages. He rose to power dramatically under the Yorkist King Edward IV, becoming Lord Chamberlain as a reward for his loyalty throughout the Wars of the Roses. After Edward's death in 1483, Hastings, on the advice of Edward's mistress

Jane Shore, refused to support his successor, Richard III. Richard had Hastings beheaded – a historical scene that was immortalized in Shakespeare's *Richard III*.

Visitors to the castle can explore the underground passage leading from the kitchen to the tower, probably created during the Civil War. There are wonderful views to be appreciated from the top of the tower.

Places to stop and rest (left) are welcome on the climb to the top of Ashby de la Zouch Castle (above)

CASTLE ACRE Norfolk

13 miles (21km) east of King's Lynn | Open daily all year | Tel: 01760 755394 | www.english-heritage.org.uk

This modest castle lies near the great Cluniac monastery of Castle Acre Priory. A castle mound was raised here by the Earls of Surrey in about AD 1080, and the first stone castle was added in the 11th or 12th century. Enormous earthworks were dug to protect it – great grassy ditches and ramparts swing around the castle, enclosing a sizeable portion of land. Look carefully at the ground in the enclosure: you might see the regular lines and grooves in the grass that are the foundations of former castle buildings.

The archaeological explorations that have taken place already on the rectangular tower that squats on the low mound at Castle Acre have given rise to some intense debate. Some people believe that the ruined walls on the northern half of the tower may once have been part of a great keep, like those at Castle Rising or Norwich, while others believe that the walls are too insubstantial to have ever supported such large buildings. Until further investigative work is carried out, the real scale of Castle Acre's walls and buildings will remain a mystery.

Right and below: Aerial views of Castle Acre mound reveal the grand scale of the enclosure

CASTLE RISING Norfolk

5½ miles (9km) north east of King's Lynn | Open daily Apr to end Oct, Wed to Sun in winter | Tel: 01553 631330 | www.castlerising.co.uk

In 1327 the unfortunate King Edward II was horribly murdered in Berkeley Castle on the orders of his wife, Queen Isabella, and her lover, Roger Mortimer. At this time, Edward's heir, Edward III, was only 15 years old, and Mortimer and Isabella were able to rule England together by manipulating the young King. This state of affairs continued for three years until Edward III began to take matters back into his own hands. Learning of the roles of his mother and Mortimer in the death of his father, Edward had Mortimer tried for treason and hanged in 1330. Isabella, as guilty as Mortimer, was spared trial and execution but was banished from the court. She spent the last 30 years or so of her life at Castle Rising, joining an order of nuns called the Poor Clares in her old age.

Although it is easy to look at the strong walls of the mighty keep at Castle Rising and imagine the fallen Queen confined, lonely and forgotten in her castle prison, there is no evidence that she was physically constrained there. In fact, there is some suggestion that she regularly toured around the area. It is more likely that Isabella's long sojourn at

Castle Rising was her own choice, and that living out her days in this peaceful corner of Norfolk was her penance for her part in the brutal murder of her husband.

There are many fascinating points about Castle Rising. As late as the 18th century, paintings of the castle show ships in the background, for when the castle was built

in the 12th century it was near the sea, or at least accessible from the sea. No visitor to Castle Rising can fail to notice the massive Norman earthworks that surround the castle. Great ditches and mounds were thrown up, with walls added later, and still today – even without the threat of archers sending out hails of arrows – the grassy earthworks are difficult to scale.

The mighty, square keep was built between 1138 and 1140, although alterations to entrances and fireplaces were carried out later, and several rooms remain in excellent condition. They include a handsome wall passage and a chapel, complete with a small wall cupboard, on one of the upper floors.

There is a well in the basement of the main tower and another in the grounds, where the remains of an 11th-century chapel have been found. Its position, half covered by earthworks, suggests that the chapel was destroyed to make way for the castle.

Above: Aerial view of Castle Rising

Left: A door into a room in the keep

Right: The keep seen from the Norman gatehouse

COLCHESTER CASTLE Essex

Colchester is the largest Norman keep ever to have been built in Britain – larger even than the enormous Tower of London. Its dimensions are staggering – 150 feet (46m) from north to south, 110 feet (34m) from east to west, and as much as 110 feet (34m) high at its corner turrets. At their splayed bases, the walls are 17 feet (over 5m) thick, but taper slightly as they rise. Because the castle layout bears some similarities to the White Tower of London, some scholars believe that both were probably designed by Gandulf, Bishop of Rochester.

Unfortunately, the keep lost its upper storeys in the 17th century. There were originally four floors, but in 1683 the castle was sold to one John Wheeley, who wanted to pull it down and sell the stones. However, the great keep proved stronger than Wheeley had anticipated, and he abandoned the demolition work after the top two floors proved something of a struggle. The idea of plundering ancient buildings arouses feelings of horror in these days of heritage conservation, but the castle itself was built from stones taken from nearby Roman ruins, and stands on the foundations of the Roman temple of Claudius.

The castle now houses a museum, displaying a wealth of archaeological finds from the city of Colchester – the first capital of Roman Britain.

Colchester Castle (top) is now a museum housing finds such as these Roman remains (above)

EASTNOR CASTLE Herefordshire

2½ miles (4km) south east of Ledbury | Open selected days Apr to Sep | Tel: 01531 633160 | **www.eastnorcastle.com**

When lawyer John Cocks, the 2nd Baron Somers, sought a rapid passage into the aristocracy, the size and splendour of the family home were seen as key indicators of status and fortune. His investment in a castle had the desired effect, for soon after its completion he became the 1st Earl Somers. Eastnor Castle was completed in 1824 for £85,923. 13s. 1d. The symmetrical design was by Robert Smirke, later the architect of the British Museum, who chose to create a Norman Revival-style fortress at Eastnor, with simple Gothic interiors. Only about half of these remain. Gothic enthusiast Augustus Pugin was commissioned to decorate the drawing room in the High Gothic style in the 1850s – the furniture, the lavish chimneypiece and the great iron chandelier are all his work. More embellishment was commissioned by Charles, the 3rd Earl Somers, over the following two decades.

Many of the items on display at Eastnor were collected during the long travels of the 3rd Earl. Something of a connoisseur, he collected Italian furniture, Flemish tapestries, Renaissance art, arms and armour. He also acquired a stunningly beautiful half-French wife, Virginia Pattle, reputedly falling in love with her when he saw her portrait by G F Watts, which is now in the Little Library.

She and her seven sisters were known as 'Pattledom', and this vivacious group was welcomed with open arms by London's artistic elite.

One of the sisters was the photographer Julia Margaret Cameron, and some of her work is also on display in the castle. The excitement and glamour of partying in London with the likes of Tennyson, Browning and Ellen Terry were a far cry from Eastnor, and Virginia rarely visited the castle, though her two daughters were brought up there.

The neatly symmetrical ivy-covered towers of Eastnor Castle, seen from the well-kept grounds

FRAMLINGHAM CASTLE Suffolk

18 miles (29km) north of Ipswich | Open most days all year | Tel: 01728 724189 | www.english-heritage.org.uk

The attractive, mellow-hued, battlemented towers and walls of Framlingham Castle have had some notable owners. It is thought that the castle that survives today was probably built by the powerful Earl of Norfolk, Roger Bigod, between about 1189 and 1200 on the site of an earlier castle. The Bigods traditionally had tempestuous relationships with their kings – Hugh Bigod supported Henry II's eldest son when he rebelled against his father in 1173, Roger Bigod II held Framlingham against King John in 1216, and Roger Bigod IV refused to go to Flanders to fight for Edward I in 1297.

Framlingham was also owned by the Mowbray family, one of whom was engaged to marry one of the unfortunate princes who 'disappeared' in the Tower of London. It was at Framlingham that 'Bloody' Mary learned that she had become Queen of England in 1553. Later, Queen Elizabeth I used the castle as a prison for priests who refused to accept the new Church of England.

Framlingham has 13 towers, all connected by walls, and a wall-walk that is open to visitors runs right round the castle, providing beautiful views over the mere.

When Framlingham was no longer used as a ducal residence, it took on several different roles through the ensuing centuries, including poorhouse (the buildings for which survive in the courtyard), parish meeting place, dance hall, courtroom, drill hall and fire station. Visitors can learn more about the castle's colourful past from the on-site exhibition 'Framlingham Castle: From Powerhouse to Poorhouse'.

Left: The mellow exterior of Framlingham Castle, a building that has had many different roles in its long history, viewed from across the mere

Top right: Decorative brickwork and attractive stone carvings do much to enhance the buildings of the 17th-century poorhouse (right)

GOODRICH CASTLE Herefordshire

6 miles (10km) north east of Monmouth | Open daily Apr to end Oct, Wed to Sun in winter | Tel: 01600 890538 | www.english-heritage.org.uk

For first-time visitors to Goodrich Castle, a great surprise lies in store. Goodrich is approached from the car park through a line of trees, and it is not until you are quite close that the full splendour of this magnificent fortress can be appreciated.

Goodrich does not possess the elegance or the picturesque quality of some castles – it was built for strength and defence. However, time has given these ruins a beauty their builders never intended, and Goodrich today is one of the castles that are most evocative of Norman dominance.

In the middle of the 12th century, the first stone building at Goodrich was raised – a sturdy, pale-red keep. It stands 60 feet (18m) high today, although it was originally taller and would probably have had battlements. In the late 13th century the de Valence family,

who owned the castle, decided to turn the simple keep into a formidable fortress. Round the keep, they built four massive walls. At three of the corners were cylindrical towers with great square bases that seem to grow out of the rock on which they are anchored. Undermining these towers would have been extremely difficult, especially as the whole castle was surrounded by a deep moat.

The fourth corner had a huge gatehouse tower that led out into the barbican. This barbican was a semicircular enclosure and forced any would-be attackers to make a right-angled turn to gain access to the castle proper. This change in direction was intended to slow the attackers down, thus exposing them to the arrows and missiles of the defenders of the castle. Gates, drawbridges and portcullises were used for the same

purpose, well provided with nearby arrow slits, so that the castle archers could fire their deadly weapons at attackers without being exposed themselves.

The gatehouse tower also housed a chapel, and the rounded end of this building can still be seen. Inside the thick walls is a range of domestic buildings that would have made castle life relatively comfortable. There was a large hall, a solar and kitchen buildings. Despite these features, Goodrich Castle was intended first and foremost as a defensive building, and, in its prime, Goodrich must have been a formidable fortress indeed.

Goodrich's square keep (left) was built for defence; features like this stained-glass window (above left) were added later. Views from the battlements (top) are superb. Battle re-enactments (above) take place here

HEDINGHAM CASTLE Essex

7 miles (11km) south west of Sudbury | Open Sun to Thu, Apr to end Oct | Tel: 01787 460261 | www.hedinghamcastle.co.uk

When the barons forced King John to sign the Magna Carta in 1215, they doubtless thought that it would bring an end to John's unpopular policies, but John was not bowed for long. Robert de Vere was the owner of Hedingham Castle and he, like other barons who sided against their king, had his castle attacked twice in what became known as the Magna Carta Wars. John died soon afterwards, and Hedingham and other properties were restored to de Vere, whose family continued to own the castle until 1703.

Today, only the keep remains of the great 12th-century fortress, but it is one of the finest in England. The exact date when it was raised is not certain, but it was probably sometime between 1120 and 1140, built by Aubrey de Vere. It has four storeys, although the second floor is twice the height of the others. This second floor forms a magnificent hall, with elegant arched windows on two levels to provide plenty of light. The whole room is spanned by a vast Norman arch, and a minstrels' gallery runs around the upper

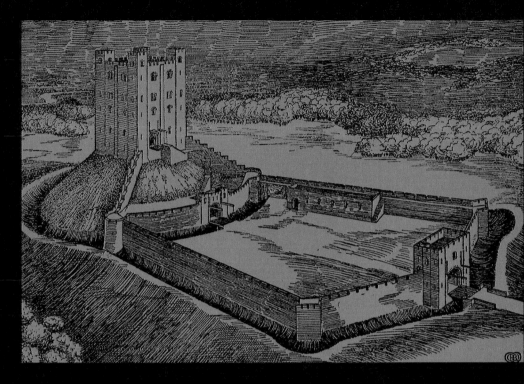

half of this splendid chamber. Like most Norman keeps, Hedingham has its main entrance on the first rather than the ground floor. This would have been accessed by a wooden staircase that could be pulled inside the castle in times of danger.

As well as the castle, there is also a beautiful Queen Anne house at Hedingham, which shares the grounds. In 2009 these grounds – which consist of formal gardens, parkland and woods – were painstakingly restored and became the subject of a Channel 4 television programme called *The Landscape Man*.

During the summer there are various events that bring the castle alive, including jousting tournaments and falconry displays as well as supercar days. The castle is also a popular place for weddings and there is accommodation in the cottage and lodge.

Left and far left: The Norman keep hides a magnificent banqueting hall and minstrels' gallery within its walls

Above: Plan of a Norman castle based on Hedingham, showing the enclosed fortified courtyard and the entrance gate leading in via a drawbridge

KENILWORTH CASTLE Warwickshire

5 miles (8km) south west of Coventry | Open daily all year | Tel: 01926 852078 | www.english-heritage.org.uk

One of Britain's mightiest keeps, built of deep-red stone, Kenilworth was the scene an important siege in English history. In 1238, a young French noble, who had claimed a tenuous hold on the earldom of Leicester, secretly married King Henry III's recently widowed sister. The young noble was Simon de Montfort, and during the next 27 years he would become one of Henry's greatest friends and most bitter enemies. Henry gave Kenilworth to his brother-in-law in 1244, but later de Montfort voiced his opposition to the absolute power of the monarchy and openly declared war on the King, making Kenilworth his rebel headquarters. At first, many nobles were struck by the sense of de Montfort's proposals, and they flocked to his cause. Even Henry's son Edward, heir to the throne of England, took de Montfort's side against his father at first. When he eventually changed sides, de Montfort imprisoned him at Kenilworth Castle. Edward escaped and played a vital role in the defeat and death of de Montfort at the Battle of Lewes in 1265.

De Montfort's supporters fled to Kenilworth, where the rebellion continued

under his son. The siege that was to follow lasted six months, and was perhaps one of the most violent ever to take place on English soil. Because the castle was protected on three sides by water, the attackers could not undermine the walls and had to concentrate instead on trying to breach the great defences of the gatehouse. Contemporary accounts tell how both the besiegers and the besieged hurled missiles at each other from great war machines. So intense was this fire that many of the stones exploded as they crashed into each other in mid air. The castle was finally overcome when the inhabitants were starved to death.

The first castle at Kenilworth was a simple mound with wooden buildings, and the magnificent keep was not raised until the 12th century. It was a massive building, with an entrance on the first floor that was protected by a substantial forebuilding. Robert Dudley, Earl of Leicester, was responsible for changing the narrow windows into large ones that would flood the upper chambers with light. Dudley was the favourite of Elizabeth I – in fact the castle was a present to him from the Queen – and he lived in constant expectation of a visit from her. He built a fine gatehouse and a graceful residential suite, intended specifically for the Queen, and also a beautiful garden in her honour. For 400 years this garden was overgrown and lost to the world. However, in 2009 it was recreated for visitors to enjoy in all its former glory.

Sir Walter Scott's novel *Kenilworth* was published in 1821. It tells of events that were supposed to have occurred during the visit of Elizabeth I to the castle in 1575.

Much has survived of this important castle. The great red keep looms powerfully over the elegant 16th-century residences, all still protected by strong walls, earthworks and the great mere.

LINCOLN CASTLE Lincolnshire

In the Bailgate area of the city centre | Open daily all year | Tel: 01522 511068 | www.lincolnshire.gov.uk/visiting/historic-buildings

In 1068 William the Conqueror ordered that a castle should be built in Lincoln on a site that had been occupied since Roman times, and 166 houses were immediately cleared away in order to make room for it. It seems inconceivable today that so many people could be uprooted from their homes at a moment's notice, but such cavalier actions on the part of landowners were not uncommon in medieval times, and the historical records of many castles tell of similar clearances.

Lincoln is one of the very few castles in Britain that has two mottes or castle mounds (Lewes in East Sussex is another). The larger of these two mottes has a 15-sided keep called the Lucy Tower, named after the mother of a 12th-century owner, Lucy, Countess of Chester. The smaller motte has a square tower with a 19th-century observatory, and huge 12th-century walls join the two mottes and enclose an area of about five acres (2ha).

Lincoln Castle was used as both a courthouse and a prison for 900 years, and one of its most interesting features today is the prison chapel, designed as a series of small cubicles so that the prisoners could not see each other or have any social contact while they worshipped. Many of the prisoners who were held at the castle were later deported to Australia or executed on the ramparts.

The castle also houses one of the four remaining originals of the Magna Carta, sealed by King John in 1215 and now on display in the new 'Charters of Liberty' exhibition. Free guided tours of the castle are offered, daily in summer and on selected days in winter.

With the Union Jack flying proudly from its Observatory Tower, Lincoln Castle still stands guard over the historic Bailgate area of the city

ORFORD CASTLE Suffolk

12 miles (19km) east of Woodbridge | Open selected days Jan to end Oct | Tel: 01394 450472 | **www.english-heritage.org.uk**

the keep survives, but it is one of the most remarkable keeps in England. It is 21-sided on the outside and round on the inside; it rises to some 90 feet (27m) in height and has five storeys. Around the rooms is a maze of passages leading to the kitchen, chapel and other chambers set within the turrets.

The castle has been well preserved, and its rooms offer a real sensation of what life would have been like in a medieval castle. Standing outside, looking up at its great creamy-grey walls, it is also easy to appreciate the size and strength of this formidable tower. Visitors can explore from the basement, where there is a vital well, through the lower and upper halls right up to the roof, where there are fabulous views seaward to Orford Ness.

The spiral stone staircase (below) inside Orford Castle (left), built by King Henry II

When Henry II came to the throne in 1154, it was quickly apparent that he had not inherited a trouble-free kingdom from King Stephen. The barons had manipulated the strife between Stephen and his rival for the throne, Matilda (Henry's mother), to accrue personal power. One such baron was Hugh Bigod, Earl of Norfolk, who owned many of the castles in the East Anglian region. Henry II knew that, in order to control the land, he must first control the castles. He took several castles that belonged to Bigod, and set about building one of his own at Orford in 1165.

Orford Castle was completed in two years, and comprised an unusual keep surrounded by walls and defensive towers. Today, only

ROCKINGHAM CASTLE Leicestershire

2 miles (3km) north of Corby | Open selected afternoons Apr to Sep | Tel: 01536 770240 | www.rockinghamcastle.com

Rockingham Castle stands on a high hill overlooking Rockingham Forest, and was a stronghold in Saxon times. William the Conqueror ordered the building of a castle here in 1066, and it had close royal links for 553 years. Henry VIII had a hunting lodge put up because the castle had fallen into disrepair, and it was the huge, imperious King who leased the castle to Edward Watson in 1544. He spent 30 years converting it into a Tudor home, dividing the Great Hall into separate rooms in the process. It was finally sold by James I for £350 to his grandson, Sir Lewis Watson, in 1619.

Sir Lewis maintained the Watsons' good relationship with the Crown, but his wife Eleanor's Parliamentarian links divided the family during the Civil War. Poor Sir Lewis tried to play safe by sending his treasure to his brother-in-law's home, Belvoir Castle, but he was unlucky: Royalists took Belvoir, while Rockingham fell to the Parliamentarians. The badly vandalized castle was returned to Sir Lewis after the war, and its restoration took up the rest of his life, and most of his son's. However, by 1669 it was complete, and much as it is today, apart from some remodelling and the addition of a tower in 1838.

Rockingham Castle's impressive self-contained layout (above) and beautifully planted grounds (right)

Visitors come in via the Servants' Hall, where some of the Norman stonework remains, and then pass along the charming cobbled 'street', once the centre of life for the self-sufficient community of the castle. The 17th-century Long Gallery is possibly the finest room in the castle, with its Chippendale furniture and fine paintings. Here, large house parties were held in the 19th century and Charles Dickens produced and acted in several of his own plays.

TATTERSHALL CASTLE Lincolnshire

Surrounded by a moat and earthworks, the great red-brick tower of Tattershall Castle stands proudly in the rolling Lincolnshire countryside. The tower is vast, its red-brown brick contrasting vividly with the bright white stone around its windows and 'machicolations' – projecting parapets with holes in them to permit objects to be thrown or fired at attackers.

Records show that nearly one million bricks were used to build the 100-foot (30m) high tower and its associated buildings. The castle was constructed between 1430 and 1450 for Ralph, Lord Cromwell, who was at that time Treasurer of England. Cromwell always intended Tattershall Castle to be an overtly aggressive statement of his power and authority, hence the formidable array of machicolations 80 feet (24m) above the ground, and the once extensive systems of water-filled moats and earthworks that surrounded the castle.

However, like many barons of his day, Cromwell wanted his home to include as many comforts as possible, as well as security, and inside the tower are six floors of fine chambers, each with small rooms in the corner towers. Visitors may well have the curious feeling that the rooms are becoming larger as they climb upwards through the castle, and this is actually the case – it was not necessary to have such thick walls in the upper floors, which were less likely to be attacked than the lower ones.

Left: The 15th-century keep of Tattershall Castle

Top right: Close-up of the windows and machicolations showing the missile holes

Right: The magnificent vaulted ceiling with a coat of arms in the centre

Far right: The main hall on the first floor. The chimneypiece is crenellated on supporting columns and bears roundels carved with Cromwell's Treasurer's purse and coat of arms

WARWICK CASTLE Warwickshire

3 miles (5km) from Leamington Spa | Open daily all year | Tel: 0871 265 2000 | www.warwick-castle.co.uk

One of the most unpopular figures in 14th-century England was the grasping Piers Gaveston. Gaveston was the son of a Gascon knight, and attracted the attention of Edward II long before he became king. Edward lavished titles and riches on his favourite, thereby antagonizing his barons into open hostility, against both Gaveston and the King himself. Several attempts were made to banish Gaveston, but none had any lasting success. Then, in 1312, desperate measures were taken when Guy, the Earl of Warwick, and other barons seized Gaveston and brought him to Warwick Castle. There, perhaps in the Great Hall, Gaveston was given a perfunctory trial and sentenced to death. He was executed on Blacklow Hill, just outside Warwick.

The powerful walls of Warwick Castle tower over the River Avon and the surrounding countryside. Because the castle has been constantly occupied since the Normans first erected a mound here, many fine buildings have been added over the centuries. Among the most magnificent are the imposing Jacobean wing and the 14th-century Guy's Tower. Inside the castle

arc many splendid rooms, including the state rooms with their lavish furnishings, as well as a tasteful tableau of wax figures that recreates a late 19th-century house party. There is an outstanding collection of arms and armour, as well as other, more recent additions, including a 'sight and sounds' exhibition called 'Kingmaker' and a new and scary Castle Dungeon, taking visitors back to 1345, when the town was gripped by the plague. For younger family members, there is an excellent, fortress-like play area and a Princess Tower. Throughout the year a number of events take place here, including falconry displays, jousting tournaments, and many tours, talks and shows.

Left: Warwick's imposing towers and ramparts

Above: The model of a knight, complete with armour and weaponry, inside the Great Hall

Overleaf: The golden facade of Warwick Castle seen from across the River Avon

NORTHERN ENGLAND | 5

Throughout Britain's stormy history, the northern part of the country has been a fortified and much disputed area. Close proximity to Scotland meant that defensive pele towers, needed for security in the wild lands of the north, became a feature of the unique rugged landscape. About 90 of these small stone buildings, with walls up to ten feet (3m) thick, square or oblong in shape, were built. Most were on the outskirts of the Lake District, but a few were within its boundaries. Designed to withstand short sieges, they usually had three storeys: a tunnel-vaulted windowless ground floor used for storage and animal housing; a hall and kitchen on the first floor; and the top floor with space for living and sleeping. Many of these towers were later built on and extended to make them comfortable dwellings. Elsewhere in the region, the grandeur of fabulous castles such as Bamburgh, crouching ferociously on its fearsome crag like a whole medieval town, or Alnwick, an intimidating sight since the Middle Ages, displays the centuries of wealth, power and influence wielded by certain families.

ALNWICK CASTLE Northumberland

20 miles (32km) north of Morpeth | Open daily Apr to end Oct | Tel: 01665 511100 | **www.alnwickcastle.com**

The clustered towers of this magnificent residential fortress have seen a good deal of action since the castle was founded in the 11th century. Its position near the border with Scotland made it vulnerable to attack from the Scots, and it played an important role in the Wars of the Roses during the 15th century. In 1172 and 1174 William the Lion, King of Scotland, laid siege to Alnwick, but on the second occasion he was surprised by reinforcements from the south and was himself taken prisoner.

Since the early 14th century, Alnwick has been the seat of the influential Percy family, Dukes of Northumberland. Although Alnwick was said to be well fortified by the 12th century, it was strengthened further in the 14th century by the Percys, who rebuilt the keep and enclosed the castle inside walls with seven semicircular towers. Sturdy gatehouses were added to both the inner and the outer walls.

After the Wars of the Roses, Alnwick began to decline. Restoration work started in the 18th century and in the 19th century it was further restored and embellished – its exterior a recreation of its medieval appearance, its interior a treasure house of works of art in the Italian Renaissance style.

Today, Alnwick Castle is the second largest inhabited castle in England. It will be recognized by many as a film location, most famously featuring as Hogwarts, the School of Witchcraft and Wizardry, in the first two Harry Potter films.

Above: The turrets of Alnwick Castle reflected in the waters of the tranquil River Aln

Left and right: Starring in the Harry Potter films has ensured Alnwick Castle's popularity with visitors

BAMBURGH CASTLE Northumberland

16 miles (26km) north of Alnwick | Open daily mid Feb to end Oct, weekends only in winter | Tel: 01668 214515 | www.bamburghcastle.com

Bamburgh's location, standing proud on a rocky promontory on the rugged Northumbrian coast, makes it one of the most spectacular of all the English castles. It is built high on a cliff, 150 feet (46m) above the North Sea. Its landward sides are protected by a forbidding display of strong walls. Bamburgh can be seen for miles, presenting a formidable obstacle to any would-be attackers.

There have been fortifications on the site for thousands of years. There was an Iron Age fort here, and the Romans, Anglo-Saxons and Vikings all left their mark. It is known that the Normans had established some kind of castle by 1095, for historical records mention that it was attacked by William II. It was also attacked by Warwick, 'The Kingmaker', during the Wars of the Roses, and much damage was done to its walls. Thereafter, it fell into disrepair, but was substantially restored during the 18th and 19th centuries.

Looking at the present-day structure of Bamburgh, it is not easy to distinguish its different periods of construction. The great tower, although altered over the years, is perhaps the most dominant feature, and there are still some traces of the original defensive walls, although these, too, have been much restored.

Like Alnwick, Bamburgh Castle has been the backdrop for many historical epics of the silver screen, including *El Cid*, *Ivanhoe*, *Becket*, *Macbeth*, *Mary Queen of Scots* and, more recently, *Elizabeth*, starring Cate Blanchett and Joseph Fiennes.

BARNARD CASTLE County Durham

20 miles (32km) west of Darlington | Open daily Apr to end Sep, weekends only Oct to end Mar | Tel: 01833 638212 | www.english-heritage.org.uk

From a small enclosure established in the late 11th century, Barnard Castle grew to cover a site of approximately 6½ acres (2.6ha). Most of this site is protected by steep cliffs, and the castle itself commands fine views across the River Tees. Sturdy walls and ditches provided additional protection.

Barnard Castle's early history revolved around its disputed ownership. It fell into Scottish hands after a successful siege by Alexander II, King of Scotland, but the powerful prince-bishops of Durham also claimed it as theirs. When King John of Scotland was deposed in 1296 the prince-bishops seized the castle, but four years later Edward I gave it to the Earl of Warwick.

Richard III owned it for a short while, and his emblem – a white boar – can still be seen carved into a window.

The most imposing part of the castle is the 13th-century Round Tower, a 40-foot (12m) structure built of fine red sandstone. It is thought that an earlier tower was demolished to make way for the current one. The Round Tower has an unusual forebuilding, or porch, which gave it additional security.

Visitors to the castle can also enjoy the sensory garden, which is filled with scented plants and tactile objects.

Barnard Castle bridge, which has spanned the River Tees since 1569, stands in front of the castle ruins

BEESTON CASTLE Cheshire

At first glance, Beeston's crumbling walls, perched on top of a rocky promontory, might appear to be too ruined to be of interest, but this once-powerful hilltop fortress has many features that are worth a second glance. It is steeped in history, not least as a key location in the Civil War, when the castle was besieged. Although the well continued to provide fresh water, the garrison was forced to surrender when it ran out of food. The well can still be seen, near one of the D-shaped towers in the inner bailey. It is 370 feet (113m) deep, and one of the deepest castle wells in the country.

Building work on the castle began in the 1220s, under the instructions of Ranulf, the influential Earl of Chester. In 1237 it passed to Henry III, who used it as a prison for luckless captives taken during his wars with Wales. Edward II added more walls and strengthened existing towers, and by the time of his murder in 1307, Beeston was virtually complete.

There is a legend that Richard II may have disposed of some of his treasure at Beeston Castle, but extensive searches have so far proved unsuccessful.

Beeston Castle, known as 'the Castle of the Rock', is famous for its spectacular views, which encompass no fewer than eight counties on a clear day

135

BOLTON CASTLE North Yorkshire

15 miles (24km) south west of Richmond | Open daily Mar to end Oct | Tel: 01969 623981 | www.boltoncastle.co.uk

Sir Richard le Scrope was Richard II's Chancellor – although he did not hold office for long, for he was outspoken about the way in which the young King squandered treasury funds. Several times he refused to set his seal to some of the King's more lavish bouts of spending. Before Scrope resigned his office at Richard's court, he was granted a licence to upgrade his manor house in Wensleydale to a castle. He hired a master mason called John Lewyn, who had also worked on the great castles of Raby and Dunstanburgh, to build him a formidable square fortress.

Bolton Castle is built in the form of a quadrangle, with strong towers at each corner. There was only one entrance into the courtyard, and that was through a vaulted passage with a portcullis at each end, also protected by a guardhouse. Inside the courtyard, every door that led into the buildings had its own portcullis. The buildings

themselves were constructed of local stone, although the decorative arches over some of the doors and windows were made of the more expensive freestone from a quarry a little farther away.

During the Civil War the castle was besieged for more than a year by Cromwell's troops, and finally taken in 1645. The castle has never been sold and remains in the private ownership of Lord Bolton, Sir Richard le Scrope's direct descendant.

The medieval gardens were reinstated in the mid-1990s and today include a herb garden, a vineyard, a maze, and a bowling green. Visitors can also enjoy falconry displays, observe wild boar feeding in the boar park, and try out their archery skills in the gardens.

Above: The castle is preserved in outstanding condition

Left and right: The interior of Bolton Castle, where Mary, Queen of Scots was held prisoner

BROUGHAM CASTLE Cumbria

The restoration of Brougham, and of the nearby Appleby and Brough Castles, is chiefly the work of the immensely rich and powerful Anne Clifford, Countess of Dorset, Pembroke and Montgomery. She wanted all three of her castles to be habitable, and spent large sums of money on making them so. She died in Brougham Castle in 1678, when she was almost 90 years old.

Brougham's origins date back to the time of Henry II when – probably around 1170 – the Great Tower was built. It was made of sandstone rubble, with more expensive, decorative cut stone at the corners and on windows and doors. The tower had buttresses on three walls, and a forebuilding on the fourth wall. It seems that the tower was originally intended to have only three storeys, but a fourth floor was added later. This later work is of a much better quality than the original, a difference that can be clearly distinguished today.

A number of other buildings were added to the keep, most notably in the 17th century by Anne Clifford. However, the splendid Great Tower remains Brougham's most impressive feature, still standing almost to its original height. The top of the keep provides fabulous panoramic views over the Eden Valley.

Lady Anne Clifford was largely responsible for making Brougham Castle into such a prestigious residence

138

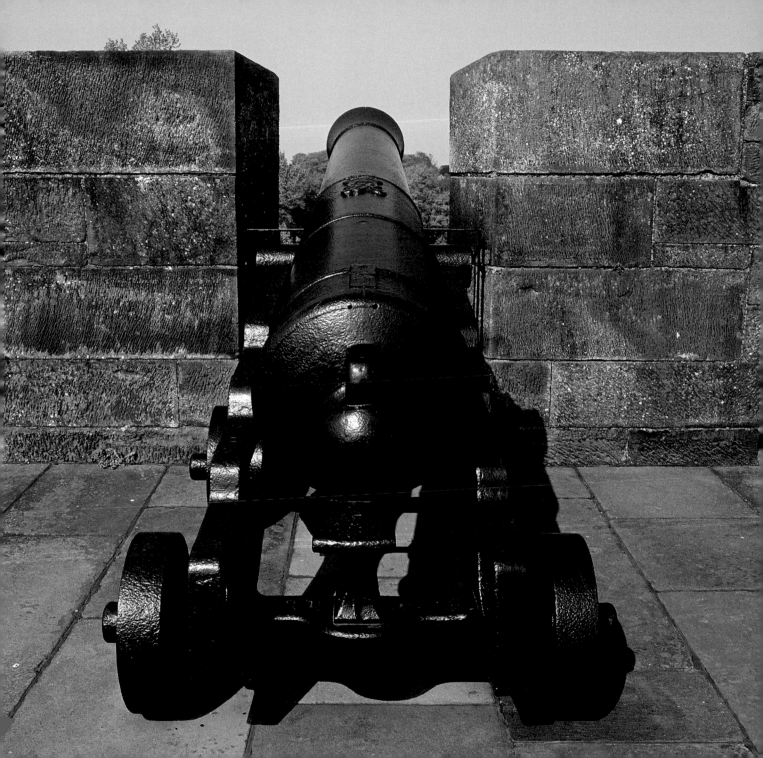

Carlisle's location so close to the Scottish border ensured that it played an important role in British history. It was held by David I and Malcolm IV, Kings of Scotland, from 1136 until 1157, and was taken back into English hands by Henry II. Another Scottish king, William the Lion, besieged the castle from 1173 to 1174.

The first castle overlooking the River Eden was nothing more than a triangular area of land encircled by a wooden fence. It was erected by William Rufus, the son of William the Conqueror, in 1092. When William Rufus was killed in a hunting accident in the New Forest, his brother Henry became king. Henry ordered that the town of Carlisle should be protected by walls and a castle. His precautions seemed well advised, because 14 years later King David attacked the border town. Despite the new fortifications the castle fell to the Scots.

Although Carlisle has been greatly altered and restored through the years, there is still much of the original to see. There is a fine 14th-century gatehouse in the inner enclosure, and visitors can still admire the buttressing on some of the walls.

Previous page: Black cannon on the battlements

Right: A medieval prisoner's stone carving of St George slaying the dragon, which was hewn into the cell wall

Below: The castle's impressive entrance gate

CHILLINGHAM CASTLE Northumberland

15 miles (24km) north of Alnwick | Open selected afternoons Apr to Oct | Tel: 01668 215359 | www.chillingham-castle.com

Sir Walter Scott may have used Chillingham as his model for Osbaldistone Hall in *Rob Roy,* for this impressive open square of a castle, with its four great corner towers, has been famous in the Borders for centuries. Held by the Grey family since they took it by force in 1245, it remains the home of their line to this day, though soldiers burned the castle's north wing in the 1940s, and rot ravaged the place until Sir Humphrey Wakefield, who married into the Grey family, began its rescue and restoration in the 1980s.

The restoration revealed more of the castle's history – including a bundle of Tudor documents hidden in a walled-up fireplace. Such discoveries help to put the long history of the Grey family into perspective. Only ten years after the original tower was captured they entertained Henry III at Chillingham, and Edward I followed in 1298. By that time the castle looked much as it does today, for Sir Thomas Grey was allowed to 'crenellate' or fortify it in 1344. A moat gave added protection and made the dungeons, with their sinister oubliette, into which prisoners were thrown and forgotten, even more dank and alarming than they are today. As one of the most important families in the north – often in rivalry with the Percys at nearby Alnwick – they helped to keep the Scots at bay. The armoured effigy of one, Sir Ralph, who died in 1443, is found on a magnificent tomb in the church at the castle's gates.

Georgian additions were made in 1753 and, after a fire in 1803, new state apartments were built in the East Range. George IV's architect from Windsor Castle, Wyatville, was called in for further modifications by Charles Grey, 5th Earl of Tankerville, who also imported the two great marble chimneypieces in the Great Hall from magnificent Wanstead House in Essex, built by architect Colen Campbell in 1720.

Outside, grass was brought up to the castle walls in the 18th century – the moat is now a huge tunnel under the south lawn. Wyatville added avenues of trees and a new formal garden on the site of the medieval tournament ground, with elaborate plantings that survived until the 1930s. Rescued from near-desolation, it currently forms a replica of an Elizabethan garden that befits one of the north's most important castles.

Older even than the castle, the 1,000-acre (405ha) park at Chillingham has been walled since 1220. Uncultivated for more than 650 years, it is still medieval in atmosphere.

A cannon in the grounds of Chillingham Castle, which is surrounded by an enormous walled park

CHIPCHASE CASTLE Northumberland

2 miles (3km) south east of Wark-on-Tyne | Open afternoons in June, other times by arrangement | Tel: 01434 230203 | www.chipchasecastle.com

If you look north from the line of Hadrian's Wall you can see Chipchase Castle, high on its plateau above the North Tyne. It is a magical mix of medieval, Jacobean and Georgian, reflecting both the turbulent history of the area and the vicissitudes of its ownership. Like many Northumbrian houses, it began life as a defensive pele tower against the Scots' frequent raids – and against the neighbours and authorities, too, for the Heron family, who owned Chipchase from 1348, were a quarrelsome lot.

How long the tower stood alone is unclear, but by 1541 a stone manor house was joined to it. It was from here that the Herons, as Keepers of Tyndale, set out on Scottish raids, sometimes in defiance of their overlords. The entire history of the family seems to have consisted of skirmish, capture and bloodshed. In 1537 John Heron was accused of murder, but was later pardoned. His son, Sir George, was killed by the Scots at Carter Bar. The Heron estates, which were considerable, were inherited by Cuthbert Heron in 1591 when he was only six. The castle's E-shaped south-east front makes it one of the north's best buildings of its time, with its four great bow windows – Victorian restorations, but very much in keeping – and the fanciful cresting over the porch tower.

Yet within 60 years of Cuthbert's confident gesture in building a new home, there was almost nothing left of the Heron fortunes. Mortgages and dowries, as well as the difficult political climate of the 17th century, had taken their toll. The family struggled on at Chipchase until 1727, when they were forced to sell. Ownership changed several times until it came to John Reed.

Reed obviously found the Jacobean house dark and gloomy, for he added sash windows and put false windows on the pele so that the south-west side of the house is symmetrical – if you can make the mental effort to ignore the turrets on the medieval tower. He transformed the interiors at Chipchase, too, with elegant plaster ceilings and fine doorcases, particularly in what is now the billiard room, where there is also a superbly carved wooden overmantle, a survivor from the previous house.

Dark, brooding and a mixture of architectural styles, Chipchase Castle was once a defensive pele tower

CLIFFORD'S TOWER North Yorkshire

York city centre | Open daily all year | Tel: 01904 646940 | www.english-heritage.org.uk

The site of Clifford's Tower was the scene of one of the most bloody incidents in York's history. In 1190 the city's Jewish population was rounded up and put into the castle, which was then burned to the ground. This unpleasant episode of English history was merely one event in a whole series of anti-Jewish riots that culminated in their expulsion from the country in 1290.

A second castle was quickly built, which involved raising the mound – originally built in about 1070 from layers of clay and marl, gravel and stones, and timber – to its present height of about 60 feet (18m). The new tower did not last long, but was blown down in a gale in 1228. Henry III ordered that a third tower should be built, and during the following quarter of a century the quatrefoil shell keep was erected on top of the mound. This unusual structure, very similar to the great tower at Etampes, near Paris, was known as the King's Tower until the 16th century. Walls and towers were also built at the bottom of the mound.

Still in its dominating position atop the grass-covered mound in the heart of old York, Clifford's Tower is a memorable landmark in this ancient city.

Clifford's Tower began as a wooden castle atop its grassy mound (left). The Jewish massacre that took place here is still remembered today (top)

DUNSTANBURGH CASTLE Northumberland

Lonely and ruined, Dunstanburgh is one of the most dramatic and atmospheric castles in Britain. Its low walls hug the rocky coastline, and only the cries of gulls and the roar of the waves disturb its peace. In order to see the castle, you must walk from the nearby village, a distance of over a mile, but the effort is worthwhile, and the absence of traffic does much to enhance the feeling of timelessness at this splendid fortress.

Dunstanburgh, unlike many other castles, was not built on the site of an earlier fortress. To understand why such a grand castle was built on such a remote part of the coast, it is necessary to look at the life of the man who built it – Thomas, Earl of Lancaster, one of the most powerful members of the aristocracy in the reign of Edward II.

The Earl and his King were constantly at loggerheads, especially over the favouritism shown by Edward to certain members of his court – and, in particular, to Piers Gaveston. Lancaster ordered Gaveston's brutal murder, and in the turmoil that followed, the Scots seized the opportunity to begin a series of raids in northern England. Dunstanburgh was therefore built both as a stronghold against a possible Scottish invasion, and as a retreat for Lancaster from the wrath of the incensed King.

The site occupied by Dunstanburgh is large, and there would have been plenty of space for local people and their livestock to take refuge from Scottish raids within the great, thick walls that swept around the site. The sea and steep cliffs provided further protection from attack on two sides.

Lancaster's impressive gatehouse was built between 1313 and 1325, and even in its ruinous state it exudes a sense of power and impregnability. It had three floors, and all the building materials appear to have been of the finest quality.

Dunstanburgh is unusual in that it acquired a second gatehouse about 60 years later. By this time, the castle had come into the hands of the Duke of Lancaster, the powerful John of Gaunt, third son of Edward III. Active in negotiations with the Scots, he doubtless saw the need for his castle to be strengthened, and as a man of influence, he travelled with a sizeable entourage, all of whom would have required accommodation.

Dunstanburgh was besieged by Yorkist armies during the Wars of the Roses, but because it was not equipped to withstand cannon bombardment, it played no active part in the Civil War.

Built as a stronghold against the Scots, lonely Dunstanburgh Castle is seen here from Embleton Bay

DURHAM CASTLE County Durham

Durham city centre | **Open afternoons in term time, mornings during vacations (guided tours only)** | **Tel: 0191 334 3800** | **www.dur.ac.uk/university-college**

On Durham City's high, rocky, natural peninsula, virtually surrounded by a loop of the winding River Wear, castle and cathedral stand side by side amidst thick woodland, presenting one of the most inspiring views in the north of England.

By the time of the Norman conquest, Durham was already a place of pilgrimage, and the bishopric of Durham was a prestigious office. It was the powerful prince-bishops who were largely responsible for building the medieval parts of the castle that survive today. Durham Castle began as a simple mound in around 1072, and it was not until the 12th century that a stone castle was built. This was pulled down in 1340, to be replaced by a grander castle, in keeping with the ever-rising status of the bishops of Durham. Although this was a castle in every sense of the word, it was also an ecclesiastical palace.

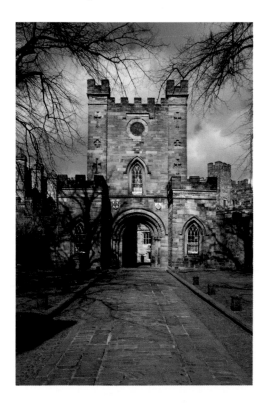

Some of the earliest work that has survived includes the beautiful chapel crypt, and one of the finest Norman archways in Britain. Between 1494 and 1500, the Bishop of Durham had some enormous kitchens installed; amazingly, these kitchens are still functional, providing meals for students, since the castle is now part of the University of Durham. The castle also shows signs of some Victorian remodelling.

As it is a working castle and home to over 100 students, entrance to the public is by guided tour only.

By day and night, Durham Castle plays an active part in the lives of students at Durham University

LINDISFARNE CASTLE Northumberland

Holy Island | Open Tue to Sun, mid Mar to end Oct (plus Mon in Aug), selected days in winter | Tel: 01289 389244 | www.nationaltrust.org.uk

Twice a day, the tide covers the ancient causeway that connects Holy Island, or Lindisfarne, to the mainland. Anyone who visits the castle and misjudges the tide must wait for several hours until the causeway opens up again, and it is not unknown for people and vehicles to be trapped by the rising tide while halfway across.

Perhaps it was this daily encroachment by the sea that attracted the early Christians to the island, for Lindisfarne has a rich history that dates back to the saints of the 7th century. In the 11th century, the Benedictines founded a monastery here, the remains of which can still be visited.

The castle, however, is comparatively modern. It was built in the 16th century, when raids by the Scots were a serious problem, and used stones taken from the recently dissolved Benedictine monastery. However, when James I of England and VI of Scotland united the two countries, the need for border defences declined and Lindisfarne was allowed to fall into disrepair. It saw action briefly in the second Jacobite uprising, when two Jacobite supporters seized control of the little fortress – and its garrison of seven men – and held it for one night.

In 1903 Lindisfarne was lovingly restored for Edward Hudson (the founder of *Country Life* magazine) by the leading country-house architect Sir Edwin Lutyens. Lutyens changed very little of the structure, but used his considerable skills to convert austere stone-vaulted ammunition rooms into comfortable living quarters. The castle is a labyrinth of small tunnels and bizarrely shaped rooms, all decorated in the style of a 17th-century Dutch mansion, with an abundance of sturdy oak furniture, brass candlesticks and attractive blue-and-white pottery.

Many of the bedrooms are tiny, and are dwarfed by the great four-poster beds that Lutyens chose. The many living rooms, most

with splendid views out to sea or down the coast, have handsome, arched fireplaces and a wealth of nooks and crannies in which Lutyens inserted small window seats. There are three floors: the upper gallery, the upper battery and the lower battery. Lutyens made use of these different levels to create an impression of size, so that the little stairways, numerous rooms and narrow passageways make the castle seem more extensive than it actually is.

Since 1968, this romantic Edwardian fortress has been in the care of the National Trust. Although no longer inhabited, it has been preserved as though it were, creating a comfortable air of timelessness.

Perched high on a rocky island crag (far left, below left and overleaf), Lindisfarne Castle has been preserved as though inhabited (left). Intricate windows, a Lutyens fireplace and a herringbone-effect floor give an intimate feel to the barrel-vaulted Ship Room (below)

MUNCASTER CASTLE Cumbria

1 mile (1.6km) east of Ravenglass | Open selected afternoons Mar to Oct | Tel: 01229 717614 | www.muncaster.co.uk

The Romans built a fort on the edge of the Lake District to protect Ravenglass harbour and the entry to Eskdale. In the Middle Ages, a castle was built on the original Roman foundations. The pele tower still survives beneath later stonework, but virtually everything we see today dates from the 1860s. Lord Muncaster, a member of the Pennington family, which came to Muncaster in 1208, commissioned Anthony Salvin to remodel both the medieval remains and a modest 18th-century house, built to his own design by a predecessor. Its situation is wonderful, with a spectacular view over the mountains from the half-mile-long terrace, and its gardens full of rhododendrons.

The Victorian building is solid and workmanlike. Two massive towers on the garden front add weight and grandeur to the outside, while inside there are individual touches, like the hall with its enclosed staircase, and the octagonal library, with a brass-railed gallery and fine vaulted ceiling. The rooms have splendid woodwork and panelling from Britain and the Continent, and carved chimneypieces (including one by Adam) brought from other houses. The furniture includes both an Elizabethan four-

The fabulous gardens at Muncaster Castle boast one of Europe's largest collections of rhododendrons

poster and a superb set of Charles II walnut settees and chairs. The house also contains a collection of glittering silverware by Paul Storr and a wonderful series of family portraits from the 17th century to the present.

King Henry VI fled to Muncaster after the Lancastrian defeat at the bloody Battle of Towton in 1461, when 30,000 men died one snowy Sunday. He was found wandering on the fells by a shepherd – the place is now marked by an 18th-century folly tower.

NEWCASTLE UPON TYNE CASTLE Tyne & Wear

Newcastle upon Tyne city centre | Open daily all year (afternoons only on Sun) | Tel: 0191 232 7938 | www.castlekeep-newcastle.org.uk

Few who travel to Newcastle by train know that the railway station lies across the site of one of the most important medieval castles in northern England. Newcastle Castle was huge, and was surrounded by great walls and defensive ditches. There were also several towers to add strength to the site, including the Black Gate, which had its own drawbridge, passage with gates, a portcullis, and a terrifying number of arrow slits.

Much of the castle has been destroyed, including the Great Hall, which was demolished in 1809. But one building that has survived is the splendid keep, its 12th-century walls rising tall and proud over the bustle of the modern city. It is built of sandstone, and the walls are generally between 15 and 18 feet (4.5m and 5.5m) thick and 65 feet (20m) high. There are five floors, although the upper one is mainly a wall gallery. One room contains a well which is 100 feet (30m) deep and lined with cut stone. The basins and pipes in this room suggest that water was probably transported to other (lower) parts of the building at one time. There is also a chapel with some fine moulded arches.

The castle's 12th-century keep (right) stands proud amid Newcastle's breathtaking new structures (below)

NORHAM CASTLE Northumberland

7 miles (11km) south west of Berwick-upon-Tweed | Open daily Apr to end Sep | Tel: 01289 304493 | www.english-heritage.org.uk

Norham was so close to the Scottish border, and was besieged or captured by either the English or the Scots with such frequency, that repairs were being carried out almost constantly from the 12th to the 16th century. In fact, the first building, founded by Flambard, Bishop of Durham in 1120, survived only 20 years before it was destroyed by the Scots.

King James IV of Scotland and his army surrounded the castle in 1513 and bombarded it with heavy artillery, destroying parts of the newly renovated Great Tower. The castle garrison surrendered, just a few days before James was killed at the Scottish defeat at the Battle of Flodden Field.

Although foundations and walls of what was once a strong fortress remain, the most imposing feature at Norham is the huge rectangular keep, its thick walls still towering up to 90 feet (27m) in places. It originally had three floors (including the vaulted basement), and most of this was completed after 1158 by the Prince-Bishop of Durham, who held the castle for many years. It passed to the Crown in 1173, and King John may have been responsible for the building of the Sheep Gate. In the 15th century, a further two floors were added.

Below and bottom left: Now a peaceful ruin, Norham Castle was once the most dangerous place in England

Bottom right: Painting of Norham by JMW Turner, c.1822

PRESTON TOWER Northumberland

1 mile (1.5km) south of Chathill | Open daily throughout the year | Tel: 01665 589227 | www.prestontower.co.uk

Some of the north's greatest houses had their origins in defensive pele towers to which, over the centuries, more comfortable quarters have been added. Preston Tower, one of 78 peles listed in 1415, is different. For more than three centuries it barely developed from its original form – and the Preston Tower that we see today is only half of that.

It was built in the 1390s by Sir Robert Harbottle, a trusted friend of Henry IV, who appointed him Sheriff of Northumberland and Constable of Dunstanburgh Castle. Robert was a contemporary of the fiery Harry Hotspur and fought alongside him against the Scots in the Battle of Otterburn in 1388. A display in the Tower illustrates life during those turbulent times. One of Robert's descendants was the gloriously named Sir Guiscard Harbottle, one of six knights killed at Flodden Field in 1513, in hand-to-hand combat with King James IV himself. The Flodden Room in Preston Tower recounts the story of Guiscard's part in the battle, and of Flodden's impact on the history and literature of Scotland and the north.

When England and Scotland were united by James I and VI in 1603, Preston Tower was partially demolished. Stones from two of its towers were used to build adjoining cottages and farm buildings, and the surviving Tower gradually decayed for the next 250 years. It was not until 1864 that Henry Baker Cresswell, whose family bought the Tower in 1861, came to the rescue. He removed the agricultural additions and built up its rear wall to make it weatherproof. He also added the clock, which he made himself. His home was the Georgian house next door, and part of the Tower was made to hold tanks of water for it, pumped from a nearby spring.

Medieval Preston Tower was a pele tower, built in the troubled years of the 1390s

PRUDHOE CASTLE Northumberland

When Prudhoe's attractive square keep was first raised, in around 1175, it was one of the first great towers to be built in Northumberland. At the same time, or a little later, a gatehouse was added, along with stone curtain walls. However, the castle's history predates the Norman keep, for in 1173 and then again in 1174, William the Lion (so called for the red lion emblazoned on his standard), King of Scotland, laid siege to the early 12th-century earthworks.

Although these sieges were ultimately unsuccessful (Prudhoe Castle was the only castle in Northumberland to resist the Scots), the threat of further attacks prompted Henry II to order a stone castle to be built.

Prudhoe was provided with a moat and drawbridge, two barbicans and a stronger gatehouse in the 13th century. A fine vaulted basement was built under the gatehouse, and a chapel was added on the first floor. The chapel had a beautiful oriel (bay) window that is thought to be one of the earliest of its kind in any English castle.

In 1381 Prudhoe passed into the hands of the influential Percy family, who at this time were still very much rivals of the other great family in the north, the Nevilles.

Prudhoe Castle (above) was one of Northumberland's earliest and strongest keeps. The gatehouse (left) may have been a slightly later addition

RABY CASTLE County Durham

The intensely romantic building we see today was begun in the 14th century. Romance was not, of course, its purpose. When the Neville family built Raby there were constant threats from Scotland, and the surrounding landscape was harsh and unwelcoming. The 30-foot (9m) curtain wall has long since gone, but the huge feudal castle, which grew gradually through the generations, retains much of its medieval impressiveness.

It was here that Richard III's mother, Cicely Neville, 'The Rose of Raby', was brought up by her father, the 1st Earl of Westmorland.

The royal connection did not help the 6th Earl, who led the Rising of the North in 1569, intended to put Mary, Queen of Scots on the throne. Defeated, he fled abroad and Raby was taken by the Crown. After more than 50 years of neglect, it was sold to the Vane family. The second Sir Henry Vane to live at Raby was executed by Charles II, but the Vanes eventually became Barons Barnard, Earls of Darlington and Dukes of Cleveland. The last duke died in 1891, and Raby is now owned by Lord Barnard.

Approached through the gatehouse is the awesome bulk of Clifford's Tower, built in about 1378. Other reminders of the original castle are Bulmer's Tower and the perfect 14th-century kitchen, with its ox-sized fireplaces, and the servants' hall. The spectacular Neville Gateway leads to the cobbled Inner Court. The long tunnel was created by John Carr when he restored and reshaped the castle in the 1760s.

The magnificent contents of the castle were all collected after the 1st Lord Barnard, furious at his son's marriage, sold everything in 1714. A favourite of many visitors is the statue of a Greek slave girl by Hiram Powers.

14th-century Raby Castle has battlemented towers, a curtain wall and a surprisingly cosy medieval kitchen

RICHMOND CASTLE North Yorkshire

4 miles (6.5km) south west of Scotch Corner | Open daily Apr to end Sep, Thu to Mon in winter | Tel: 01748 822493 | www.english-heritage.org.uk

Below: Surrounding houses dwarfed by the castle keep

Right: The sheer sides of the castle seen from the banks of the River Swale

Below right: The vaulted ceiling inside the keep

Commanding a powerful position on the banks of the River Swale, this mighty fortress was never put to the test, for Richmond has never seen military action. Its location is superb, with steep cliffs protecting one side, and thick walls defending the other sides.

The Normans started constructing a castle here in the 1080s, and it is thought that Scolland's Hall – a fine, two-storeyed hall with typical round-headed windows – is one of the earliest stone-built halls in England. The towers at Richmond have romantic names: Robin Hood Tower, now in ruins, is said to have been the prison of William the Lion, King of Scotland; the Gold Hole Tower may have a poetic ring to its name, but it was actually the latrine tower, complete with pits at its base, spanned by an interesting 11th-century arch. By far the largest building of the entire complex is the keep. It started life as a gatehouse in the 11th century, but in the mid-12th century it was extended upwards to a height of 100 feet (30m). Straight flights of stairs ran between the floors, rather than the traditional spiral stairways.

RIPLEY CASTLE North Yorkshire

The colourful and eccentric Ingilbys have lived at Ripley Castle since 1308/9 when Thomas married Edeline Thweng, heiress to the estate. Despite attaining high office in the judiciary, he is best remembered for saving the life of Edward III when he was attacked by a wounded boar while hunting.

This act of valour won Thomas a knighthood, but the Ingilby's Catholicism cost them dear. Sir William joined the conspirators in the 'Pilgrimage of Grace' and was saved from execution by Henry VIII only because he had advised against taking action. His son, Francis, trained as a Jesuit priest in the seminary at Rheims, returning to England in 1584; captured two years later, he was convicted of treason and hung, drawn and quartered at York. Beatified in 1987, he is the only Ingilby likely to become a saint. His brother, William, narrowly avoided execution for treason when he was unjustly implicated in the Gunpowder Plot.

Loyalty to the Crown proved equally hazardous: Sir William was fined over £700 for 'delinquency' in supporting Charles I during the Civil War, and his son briefly fled into exile with James II. More prosaically, in 1794, the then baronet and his wife abandoned their six small children by escaping to Europe to avoid their creditors. It was ten years before he could pay them off and return home.

The medieval fortifications of Ripley Castle were built to provide protection from marauding Scots, but later baronets added a 16th-century tower and an 18th-century mansion house. Designed by John Carr of York, the house is the most elegant part of the castle, with furniture by Chippendale (whose father was a joiner on the Ripley estate) and Hepplewhite. The continental residence of various Ingilbys, both enforced and voluntary, is reflected in the Venetian chandeliers and Italian plasterwork ceilings and statuary. Most fascinating of all are the tower rooms: the library, with its huge 18th-century table, 5,000 books and the 1386 foundation charter of Mount Grace Priory; above it, the Tower Room, with a fabulous plasterwork ceiling, where James I slept in 1603; and, on the third storey, the gem of the castle, the perfectly preserved Knight's Chamber of 1555. Interesting features include a priest hole hidden behind the panelling and the door leading to a spiral staircase that has a prominent false handle to delay attackers.

Romantic Ripley Castle has a waterfall in its grounds

158

SCARBOROUGH CASTLE North Yorkshire

East of Scarborough town centre | Open daily Apr to end Sep, Thu to Mon in winter | Tel: 01723 372451 | www.english-heritage.org.uk

Unlike most medieval castles, Scarborough saw action in World War I, when shells from German battleships damaged its walls. Historical records indicate that this was not the first time that the castle had come under attack, and several English kings received bills for repairs, from Henry II to James I.

The rocky headland on which the castle was built had been an important site for hundreds of years before the Normans came, the cliffs providing a natural defence, which was further strengthened by curtain walls. The keep, now in ruins, was built by Henry II on the site of an earlier tower. It was originally 100 feet (30m) high, and had walls that were up to 12 feet (3.7m) thick. There was also a forebuilding that has not survived.

Scarborough was again attacked in 1536 during the 'Pilgrimage of Grace', a rebellion against Henry VIII that protested against issues such as the dissolution of the monasteries, the Reformation and a whole host of economic grievances. The rebellion, mainly in the north, was led by Robert Ashe. Henry VIII agreed to listen to the complaints of the leaders, but as soon as the rebels began to disband, he had 230 of them, including Ashe, executed.

Scarborough Castle on its rocky headland (right) and ravaged by storms in a 19th-century engraving (below)

SIZERGH CASTLE Cumbria

🦁 3 miles (5km) south of Kendal | Open selected afternoons Mar to end Oct | Tel: 01539 560951 | www.nationaltrust.org.uk

There is a great 14th-century tower at the heart of Sizergh Castle, the original part of a building that had the misfortune to be within a wide band of the country that, at that time, frequently changed hands between England and Scotland. This pele tower is still recognizable, but a great deal of building was done during Tudor times, extending the castle to the north and west and adding a great chamber over the old hall.

Most of the interior now reflects this time of prosperity and expansion, with superb oak panelling and some outstanding carving. The intricately inlaid panelling of the Inlaid Chamber was sold in 1891 to the Victoria and Albert Museum, but they have kindly loaned two panels back to Sizergh so that visitors can imagine how the room would have looked in its heyday. The museum also loaned the inlaid bed, which had been made to match the room.

In 1239 the heiress of Sizergh Castle married into the Strickland family, and Stricklands still live in the castle today, although they gave it to the National Trust in 1950. Their occupancy of the castle was unbroken except for a short time when the family accompanied King James II into exile. Their support of the Stuart cause is reflected in many of the portraits in the house.

Sir Thomas Strickland had the honour of carrying the banner of St George – England's premier banner – to the Battle of Agincourt in 1415, in which the English were victorious against the French.

Left: The crenellated towers of Sizergh Castle are set in beautiful grounds. The building is medieval, with Elizabethan additions

Right: Inside the Banqueting Hall at Sizergh Castle, the refectory table dates from the period of James I and the oak chairs and carved oak forms are 16th century. The pewter tableware is 17th and 18th century, and the wooden floor was hewn by an adze

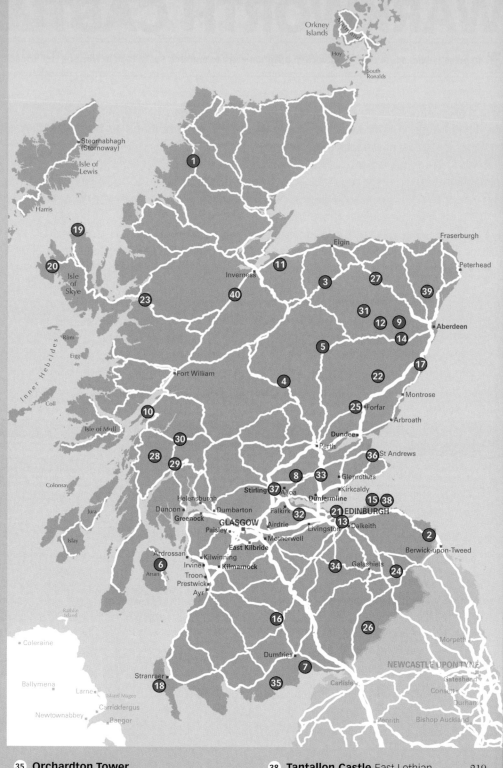

SCOTLAND & THE BORDERS | 6

When King Alexander III of Scotland died in 1286, leaving no heir, Edward I attempted to bring Scotland under English control. Edward died in 1307, but his son, Edward II, continued his aggressive policies. In the following decade, Scottish castles changed hands with bewildering rapidity. Although Robert the Bruce had suffered a humiliating defeat at the Battle of Methven in 1306, his fortunes changed in 1307 and he became one of Scotland's most dynamic kings, taking back from the English all the castles Edward had won.

Stirling was, perhaps, the castle that faced the greatest number of changes. Edward took it in 1296 and Wallace took it back in 1297; Edward captured it in 1298 and Wallace recaptured it in 1299, holding it until Edward reclaimed it in 1304. It remained in English hands until the great Scottish victory at Bannockburn delivered it back to Bruce in 1314. Many castles changed ownership in this way – Caerlaverock, Dirleton, Edinburgh, Hermitage, Kildrummy and Urquhart all had English and Scottish occupying forces in them at least twice during the period from 1297 to 1314. When Wallace or Bruce seized a castle from the English, they knew that their hold would be temporary, and consequently they would 'slight' the building to prevent future use as an English garrison. Caerlaverock suffered this fate. Bruce also slighted Edinburgh, though the damage did not deter the English king, who, within a few years, had repaired it and had even planted a garden in anticipation of a long stay.

Castles survived the rollercoaster of the Wars of Independence to varying degrees. Some, like Edinburgh and Stirling, continued to be of service to the Scottish nation, while others gradually fell into disrepair.

ARDVRECK CASTLE Highland

26 miles (42km) north east of Ullapool | Open access all year | www.visitourscotland.co.uk/ardvreck

When Civil War broke out in England in 1642, Scotland was inevitably drawn into the conflict. Two of the main protagonists in the north were Archibald Campbell, Marquess of Argyll, and James Graham, Marquess of Montrose. Montrose remained loyal to the King, while Argyll declared for Parliament. After the execution of Charles I in 1649, Montrose fled the country, but returned a year later. He was captured by the Laird of Assynt, who held him in Ardvreck Castle until he could be safely handed over to Cromwell's forces. Montrose was hastily executed in the same year, while his rival, Argyll, was executed after the Restoration of the monarchy in 1661.

The small 16th-century tower house is now a ruin, perched on a rocky peninsula that juts out into Loch Assynt. It was a simple structure – rectangular, with a staircase turret on the south-east corner. The basement had three chambers with vaulted roofs. One of the chambers is little more than a passage, but the gun loops pierced in its outer wall suggest that it could have been used to defend the castle. When observing Ardvreck Castle, visitors may notice some other ruins nearby. These are the remains of Edderchalder House, a 17th-century mansion.

The castle can be seen from the A837, and is best admired from a distance – tread very carefully if you visit the ruins, as a lot of stones are loose.

Left and below: Ardvreck Castle on the shore of Loch Assynt, with the Quinag mountain behind

AYTON CASTLE Border

Though Ayton Castle is a true creation of the Victorian age, there has been a castle on the site since Norman times. In the 15th century it was owned by the Homes family, but was confiscated by the Crown because of their support for the Stuart cause. In the mid-18th century, the estate was acquired by James Fordyce, who was the Scottish Commissioner for Lands and Forests. At that time the estate was important and rich enough to instigate the removal of Ayton village to a more distant location. That castle was completely devastated by fire in the early years of the 19th century.

The basis of the Ayton Castle we see today was commissioned by the 19th-century owner, William Mitchell-Innes, who chose James Gillespie Graham to create for him a suitably grand, though not excessively large, residence: he was a practical man, who saw no need for rooms he could not utilize. His son, however, had a much larger family and found it necessary to extend Ayton soon after he inherited it in 1860.

In addition to adding new rooms, including an attic suite of nurseries, the castle was splendidly redecorated and the rich plasterwork of the ceilings remains a particularly fine feature.

In 1886 the castle was sold to Henry Liddell, a Northumberland landowner, and the widow of his grandson, David Liddell-Grainger, is the present owner.

**Above: Ayton Castle viewed from the village road
Right: The library and (far right) the drawing room**

BALLINDALLOCH CASTLE Moray

29 miles (47km) north east of Aviemore | Open Sun to Fri, Apr to end Sep | Tel: 01807 500205 | www.ballindallochcastle.co.uk

One of the most beautiful castles in Scotland, Ballindalloch nestles at the heart of the picturesque Spey valley, with the majestic mountains of the Cairngorm massif rising to the south, and the waters of the rivers Spey and Avon flowing through the grounds. Known, fittingly, as 'the Pearl of the North', Ballindalloch has been home to the Macpherson-Grants since 1546 and is one of the few privately owned castles to have been lived in continuously by the original family.

Built originally in the traditional Z plan, Ballindalloch illustrates the development from the fortified tower house of the 16th century to the elegant Highland country house so admired by the Victorians. The house today is very much a lived-in home, filled with family memorabilia, an important collection of 17th-century Spanish paintings and some fine furniture.

The Hall, designed by architect Thomas MacKenzie in the 1850s, has an unusual umbrella design and fan vaulting. Of interest in this room are a Sheraton corner cupboard by Ridgeway, c.1820; a fine *bureau plat* (writing table) of Louis Quinze period; and a set of Scottish chairs made in Chinese Chippendale style, with unusual carvings of bells. Some 18th-century pistols hang over the fireplace; Scottish dirks on display were used for hunting or dealing with enemies. The Dining Room – originally the Great Hall of the castle – was redesigned during the 1850 renovations and panelled in American pine. The magnificent fireplace, with the Macpherson and Grant coats of arms above, was installed at the same time.

In the grounds are a superb rock garden, with tumbling spring water, laid out in 1937 by the 5th Baronet, and a walled garden, redesigned in 1996 to celebrate the castle's 450th anniversary – a haven of beauty.

Ballindalloch Castle is set in magnificent grounds between the rivers Spey and Avon

In 1269 affairs of state forced David, Earl of Atholl, to spend a considerable amount of time in England. While he was away, his neighbour, John Comyn, began to build a castle on Atholl's land, causing Atholl to complain to King Alexander III. This early tower is now incorporated into a much bigger castle, but is still called Cummings (or Comyn's) Tower.

The Earls and Dukes of Atholl were prominent men in Scottish history. The simple tower house was extended and rebuilt over the centuries according to the needs of its different owners. In the English Civil War, Blair Castle, then a fortress with good defences, was captured by Cromwell's forces. In 1745 it was besieged by the Jacobites, in what was probably the last siege to take place in Britain.

Most of the castle as it is seen today dates from the 18th century. It is a splendid palace, its gleaming white walls contrasting starkly with the rich woodland in which it stands. Many richly furnished rooms are open to the public, and some contain objects of great historical significance, including two cannons from an Armada galleon and an original copy of the National Covenant of 1638.

A more recent addition to the castle's rich history is Blair's private army. When Queen Victoria came to stay at the castle in 1844, some 200 Athollmen formed a royal bodyguard, so enchanting the young Queen that she presented them with their colours in the following year. As the only private army in the country, the Atholl Highlanders, still recruited largely from the estate, exist today as a ceremonial private bodyguard.

Above: Amid rolling green countryside, Blair Castle's gleaming white walls can be seen for miles

Right: The entrance hall is hung with weaponry

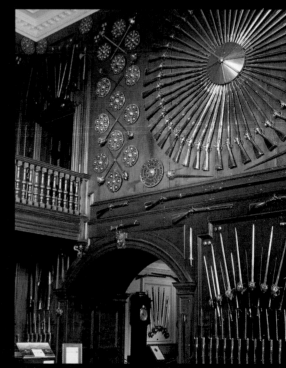

BRAEMAR CASTLE Aberdeenshire

½ mile (0.8km) east of Braemar | Open weekends Apr to end Oct and Wed in Jul and Aug | Tel: 01339 741219 | www.braemarcastle.co.uk

Its strategic location on the main route through the mountains has meant a turbulent history for Braemar Castle; not only has it changed hands several times, but it has also been burnt out and deserted, and used as a garrison fort for Hanoverian troops determined to crush any further Highland rebellion. Later fitted out in the best 19th-century traditions of elegance, style and comfort, it is today the delightful family home of the Farquharsons of Invercauld.

The castle was started in 1628 by John Erskine, Earl of Mar, to fend off his belligerent neighbours along the valley – the Farquharsons, the Gordons and the Forbes – and its original structure as an L-shaped tower house can still be seen clearly. The Earl of Mar was an important figure in Scottish politics, holding the position of High Treasurer of Scotland and guardian to the young King James VI (later James I of England).

The first serious conflict arose in 1689. While the current Earl of Mar supported the Hanoverian government, his neighbours the Farquharsons favoured the doomed Jacobite cause, and rallied to support the stand made by John Graham of Claverhouse ('Bonnie Dundee'). The Hanoverian troops on the trail of Claverhouse, under General Mackay, stopped off at Braemar Castle, but were routed by the Farquharsons in a surprise night attack. The Farquharson leader, John, 'The Black Colonel', ordered the castle to be burned, to prevent its further use by government troops, and for 60 years it remained a forlorn, burnt-out shell.

Braemar Castle was rebuilt, and remains one of the best examples of a Hanoverian fort. Turrets were extended, a rectangular rampart was constructed with projecting salients to make the classic eight-point star shape, and the interior was worked on by the two young sons of the great architect William Adam, one of whom, Robert, would later outstrip his father's fame.

Braemar Castle, seat of the Farquharson clan, was a 17th-century hunting lodge and Hanoverian garrison

BRODICK CASTLE
Isle of Arran

After Robert the Bruce's defeat at Methven in 1306, he fled to Brodick Castle on the Isle of Arran. It was here that he is supposed to have waited for the beacon to be lit on the mainland, telling him the time was ripe to begin afresh his war with the English King Edward I. Within a year, Edward was dead and Bruce was establishing himself as King of Scotland.

Nowadays, little remains of the 14th-century castle which, according to contemporary accounts, was 'levelled to the ground' in 1455 by the Earl of Ross. It was rebuilt, but in 1544 the Earl of Lennox destroyed it, acting on the orders of Henry VIII. The castle was repaired again in the 1630s so that it could be garrisoned for Charles I, but these buildings were largely swept away for the Scots baronial mansion that was designed by James Gillespie Graham in the 19th century.

The mansion is an elegant red sandstone building, displaying clusters of chimneys, gables and towers, and nestling comfortably in its attractive gardens. A number of rooms are open to the public, displaying a diverse

Brodick's 13th-century fortified tower was developed in the 16th century and extended in the 17th century

collection of sporting trophies and some excellent paintings.

The castle gardens are also well worth exploring. They extend from seashore to mountain top and include dramatic gorges, waymarked trails in native woodland, a fabulous rhododendron garden that contains flowers most of the year, and a formal walled garden. Brodick is unique in being the only island country park in Britain.

CAERLAVEROCK CASTLE
Dumfries & Galloway

12 miles (19km) south east of Dumfries | Open daily all year | Tel: 01387 770244 | www.historic-scotland.gov.uk

The imposing gatehouse at Caerlaverock Castle is so similar to those designed by Edward I's master castle-builder, James of St George, that it is often suggested that this was an English, rather than a Scottish, fortress. The high walls, with their massive round towers, two moats and high ramparts, are very similar to the concentric castles built by Edward in Wales, such as Beaumaris and Harlech; but, unlike any other castle in Britain, Caerlaverock is triangular. It has three walls: two protected by an arm of the sea that swings out round the back of the castle, and the third by moats, earthworks and the great gatehouse.

Caerlaverock was built in the late 13th century, and exchanged hands several times when Edward invaded Scotland. Edward laid siege to it in 1300, after which it was besieged another four times during its eventful history. Often, if the Scots took a castle but were unable to hold it, they would destroy it so that the English could not use it. This happened to Caerlaverock in 1312, and it was almost completely rebuilt in the 15th

Right: Cannons deter visitors to the castle gatehouse
Below: A 19th-century engraving of the castle

century. Rebuilding followed the previous plan, although gun ports were added, and the great gatehouse was strengthened to withstand cannon fire.

In the centre of the castle courtyard stands the attractive Nithsdale Lodging – a 17th-century residence built by Robert Maxwell, the 1st Earl of Nithsdale. The facade is embellished with ornate Renaissance stone carvings, which contrast beautifully with the stark medieval castle walls.

Visitors to the castle can also enjoy a nature trail and a siege warfare exhibition.

Above: The castle ruins are surrounded by a moat
Right: Carving and embellishment inside the castle

CASTLE CAMPBELL Clackmannanshire

10 miles (16km) east of Stirling | **Open daily Apr to end Oct, Sat to Wed in winter** | **Tel: 01259 742408** | **www.historic-scotland.gov.uk**

The original name of this stronghold was 'the Castle of Gloume', but the 1st Earl of Argyll disliked the name and changed it by an Act of Parliament in 1489 to the less dismal Castle Campbell. The castle stands on a rocky spur of land between two streams, rather mournfully named the Burn of Care and the Burn of Sorrow.

It is not known exactly when the first castle was raised here, but the earliest surviving building dates from the end of the 15th century. This fine tower is in an excellent state of preservation, and stands about 60 feet (18m) high to its parapets. It has four storeys, three of which have handsome vaulted ceilings, and there was a pit prison in the basement. During the 16th century the simple tower house was extended to form a quadrangle, although the castle's position on a rocky knoll restricted further development.

During the English Civil War, Castle Campbell's owner, the Earl of Argyll, sided firmly with Oliver Cromwell's Parliamentarian forces. In 1654 Castle Campbell was burned down by the Royalists, and in 1661 the Earl of Argyll was executed. Since then, much of the castle has remained derelict, although the splendid tower house and the east wing were used as a residence by the Argylls until the early 19th century.

Castle Campbell stands on a narrow ridge, overlooked by a crescent of the Ochil Hills

CASTLE FRASER Aberdeenshire

16 miles (26km) west of Aberdeen | Open daily Jul and Aug, Wed to Sun in Apr, May, Jun, Sep and Oct | Tel: 0844 493 2164 | **www.nts.org.uk**

Castle Fraser is a handsome baronial castle dating back to the 15th century, and was the ancestral home of the Fraser family. The elegant tower house contains an extraordinary wealth of treasures, not only in terms of displays, but also architecturally. Highlights include the Great Hall, dating back to the 1400s, family portraits, fine furniture, an original library and a grand room with 18th-century embroideries. Among the most intriguing items in the exhibition of Fraser family history are two bullets and a wooden leg. These date from the Peninsular War of 1812, in which Colonel Charles Mackenzie Fraser lost his leg. One of the bullets is labelled 'head' and the other 'leg'.

Another curious feature is the 'lug-gie', or secret listening point between the hall and the chamber above. This was a small cubby-hole that was dug into the thickness of the

Castle Fraser (right) is a vast baronial castle. This coat of arms emblem (below) was hewn into the wall

wall, and concealed behind a window shutter. Eavesdroppers could remove the stone slab, slip into the cubby-hole, and listen to what was being said in the hall below.

Even though the two 17th-century wings that stretch out on either side of the original tower to form a courtyard are closed to

athe public, there is still plenty to see at this vast castle, and the grounds are well worth exploring too. There are signposted walks in mature woodland, an 18th-century walled garden and a 'flight pond' – a haven for wildlife where you may spot otters, rare dragonflies and red kites.

CASTLE STALKER Argyll & Bute

18 miles (29km) north of Oban | Open selected days in May, Jul, Aug and Sep | Tel: 01631 730354 or 07789 597442 | www.castlestalker.com

Standing on a tiny island in Loch Laich, this small tower house can be seen from the road that runs from Ballachulish towards Oban. It bears some resemblance to the castle of Eilean Donan, since both are set in lonely sites, surrounded by water, and are simple tower structures.

Historically, it would appear that access to Castle Stalker has always been by boat, and no causeway has ever been built to make it more easily accessible, but at low tide it is possible to wade across the shallow waters of the loch.

The castle itself is a rectangular tower, about 45 feet (14m) by 36 feet (11m) at its base, and was built in the 16th century. The fact that its walls were nine feet (2.7m) thick, coupled with the inaccessibility of its site, meant that it was fairly well protected against would-be invaders. The entrance was at first-floor level, and access originally would have been up wooden steps, or a ladder that could have been drawn up into the tower in times of danger. The stone stairway that can be seen today was a later addition.

Castle Stalker became derelict after the second Jacobite rising in the 18th century, and was restored only relatively recently

CAWDOR CASTLE Highland

6 miles (10km) south west of Nairn | Open daily May to end Sep | Tel: 01667 404401 | www.cawdorcastle.com

Cawdor Castle has a violent history. It was home to the legendary Thanes of Cawdor, who played an active role in Scottish politics throughout the centuries, but were plagued by ill-fortune. The 9th Thane was branded on the hip with a red-hot key as a child, and both the 4th and the 11th Thanes were brutally murdered.

Thanks to William Shakespeare, Cawdor is associated in the minds of many with Macbeth's murder of King Duncan, but as Macbeth lived during the 11th century, and Cawdor was not built until the 14th century, the link between Duncan's bloody murder and Cawdor Castle may be poetic licence.

Nevertheless, the somewhat sinister appearance of the austere tower and battlements make it easy to imagine why Shakespeare chose it as the location for his grim tale of madness and regicide.

The keep dates from the 15th century, and is a forbidding grey tower with walls 11 feet (over 3m) thick in places, once surrounded by a deep ditch. The later buildings sprout an attractive arrangement of steep-sided roofs, crow-stepped gables and small turrets dating from the 17th and 19th centuries. Inside, visitors can explore parts of the keep and rooms in the later buildings. There is a fine 17th-century kitchen displaying an array of antique household utensils, and bedrooms containing an elegant Georgian bed and an exquisite Flemish tapestry.

There are three interesting gardens in the grounds – a walled garden, a flower garden and a wild garden. In addition, there is the Big Wood, which contains a huge range of native woodland trees and rare lichens.

The drawbridge and entrance to Cawdor Castle (left) has an ornate coat of arms over the gate (right)

Cawdor has three different gardens (above right) and a series of splendid rooms such as the Tapestry Bedroom or 'Crimson Chamber' (far right)

CRAIGIEVAR CASTLE Aberdeenshire

7 miles (11km) south of Alford | Open daily Jul and Aug, Fri to Tue in May, Jun and Sep | Tel: 0844 493 2174 | www.nts.org.uk

Standing amid attractive woodland, and built of a delicate rose-pink granite, Craigievar is one of the most romantic of the 17th-century Scottish tower houses. Although it is perhaps one of the most lavish and ornate, it was also one of the last of its kind to be built. Within two decades of its completion the Civil War broke out in England, and many castles and fortified houses came under devastating bombardment from cannons. Since it was no longer possible to build a house that could withstand such firepower indefinitely, fortresses became obsolete, and in their place came the elegant Classical-style mansions and townhouses that categorize the 18th century.

No expense was spared by the wealthy merchant, Sir William Forbes, who built Craigievar in the 1620s. It was he who ordered the decorative turrets that adorn each corner and the elegant carvings high up on the walls.

Inside the castle are more reminders of Forbes' wealth. Many rooms have retained their impressive Renaissance plaster ceilings, and the elegant hall has arcaded panelling with a royal coat of arms over the granite fireplace. This magical L-plan castle is now owned by the National Trust for Scotland. Artificial lighting has never been installed at the castle, in accordance with the Forbes-Sempill family's wishes, so it's best to visit on a bright day.

Craigievar Castle, reminiscent of gothic fantasy, is full of charming detail like this staddle-stone (right)

CRAIGMILLAR CASTLE Midlothian

2 miles (4km) south east of Edinburgh | Open daily Apr to end Oct, Sat to Wed in winter | Tel: 0131 661 4445 | **www.historic-scotland.gov.uk**

Buildings from four different periods make up the splendid ruins at Craigmillar. A simple L-plan tower house made of red-grey sandstone was built here in the late 14th century. In the 1420s, this sturdy tower was fortified by the addition of a wall, 28 feet (8.5m) high with round towers at the corners, which ran all the way around it. Another set of walls and other buildings were added in the 16th and 17th centuries, including a chapel and kitchens, the remains of which can still be seen.

Although Craigmillar is a good example of a late medieval fortress, it is perhaps better known for its role in history. The first significant bloody act at Craigmillar was the murder of the Earl of Mar by a jealous brother in 1477. The castle was attacked and seriously damaged by the Earl of Hereford for Henry VIII in 1544, but was sufficiently repaired for Mary, Queen of Scots to retreat there following the murder of a favourite secretary in 1566. While Mary grieved for her loss, her noblemen plotted revenge. It is not known whether Mary was a party to the plot, but a pact was signed that resulted in the murder of Mary's estranged husband, Lord Darnley. While convalescing from an illness, his house was blown up. When his body was recovered, it was found that Darnley had been strangled before the explosion.

Peaceful grazing outside Craigmillar Castle in the 21st century (top), and in a 19th-century engraving (above)

184

CRATHES CASTLE Aberdeenshire

🦁 3 miles (5km) east of Banchory | Open daily Apr to Oct, weekends only in winter | Tel: 0844 493 2166 | **www.nts.org.uk**

Crathes Castle is said to have a ghost. The story goes that the illegitimate child of a lady was murdered and buried under the hearth in the Green Room. It is said that moans and wails are sometimes heard echoing through Crathes' lonely halls, and that a mysterious green light has been seen by some visitors to the castle. Whether or not the story is true, a great deal more is on offer here.

Crathes was built in the 1550s for the wealthy Burnett family, and when the splendid multi-storeyed building proved too small for Thomas Burnett and his 21 children, some time in the early 18th century, he set about enlarging and restoring the castle. The outcome was the beginning of the stately gardens that still surround the house, and an elegant building known as the Queen Anne Wing. Unfortunately, this was gutted in a serious fire in 1966, although the original L-plan tower escaped serious harm.

Crathes Castle has been restored by the National Trust for Scotland. In the same mould as Glamis and Craigievar, it is made from rose-shaded granite and capped with attractive clusters of turrets and chimneys.

Crathes Castle has a croquet lawn and elegant topiary (previous page), a profusion of colourful borders (above), and millstones at the doorway (right)

186

DIRLETON CASTLE East Lothian

🦁 **11 miles (18km) north east of Edinburgh** | **Open daily all year** | **Tel: 01620 850330** | **www.historic-scotland.gov.uk**

This sturdy castle was raised in the 13th century, probably on the remains of an earlier fortress. The principal building was the impressive three-storeyed round keep or 'drum' tower, supported by a complex arrangement of other towers and walls. In the 14th and 15th centuries the castle was considerably enlarged to include a chapel with a prison beneath, and a pit prison hewn from the rock below that. Although a ruin, Dirleton still presents an imposing face to the world, and crossing the modern wooden footbridge to the great gatehouse it is easy to appreciate the difficulties faced by any would-be attacker.

Dorothea, wife of the rebellious Earl of Gowrie, was probably one of the saddest residents of Dirleton Castle. Her husband was executed in 1585 after a plot to seize Stirling Castle was discovered, and all his lands and castles were taken by King James VI, leaving

A murder hole (right), through which missiles could be thrown or boiling oil poured on attackers of the castle

Dorothea and her 15 children poverty-stricken. The King granted Dirleton Castle to Gowrie's great rival, the Earl of Arran, who kept it until the castle and its lands were restored to Dorothea almost two years later. Then, in 1600, two of her sons were involved in the mysterious 'Gowrie Conspiracy', when it was alleged that they tried to kill the King. Although the maiming of the corpses of Dorothea's sons was very public, details of the entire affair remained secret.

Right: Inside Dirleton Castle's thick walls
Below: The modern footbridge leading to the gatehouse

DRUMLANRIG CASTLE Dumfries & Galloway

8 miles (13km) north of Dumfries | **Open daily Mar to end Aug** | **Tel: 01848 331555** | **www.drumlanrig.com**

Drumlanrig was a Douglas stronghold as far back as the 14th century and Sir James Douglas was the right-hand man of Robert the Bruce, King of Scotland. Indeed, the family crest of a winged heart surmounted by Bruce's crown, which appears throughout the house, stems from that alliance.

The present palatial structure was built around the original castle by William Douglas, 1st Duke of Queensberry. An impressive horseshoe staircase and colonnaded archway lead up to the castle entrance. Masterpieces such as Leonardo da Vinci's *Madonna with the Yarnwinder*, Hans Holbein the Younger's *Sir Nicholas Carew* and Rembrandt's *Old Woman Reading* adorn the Staircase Hall.

A tour of the castle reveals room after room of priceless works of art, from the exquisite Grinling Gibbons carvings and Meissen Monkey Band in the drawing room to the Dutch and Flemish paintings in the Boudoir. From the early Douglases to the present-day guardians of the estate, the family motto of 'Forward' has true meaning. Rural land management and woodland conservation combined with a shrewd business sense will ensure that the stately Drumlanrig Castle and all its treasures can be enjoyed for many generations to come.

Drumlanrig Castle has played host to many celebrity guests throughout its history, from Mary, Queen of Scots to the first moon-walking astronaut, Neil Armstrong. No-one's visit has been more commemorated, however, than that of Prince Charles Edward Stuart, Bonnie Prince Charlie. The bedroom that he occupied on his retreat northwards on 22 December 1745 has been dedicated to his memory. A pastel of the Prince and an oil painting of his father hang either side of one window, and several personal items, including his money box, rings, some miniatures and a camp kettle, are on display.

Drumlanrig Castle is a fine example of late 17th-century Renaissance architecture

DUNNOTTAR CASTLE Aberdeenshire

1 mile (1.6km) south east of Stonehaven | Open daily all year | Tel: 01330 860223 | **www.dunnottarcastle.co.uk**

On the rugged coastline south of Aberdeen a great stack of rock projects into the stormy North Sea, topped by a jumbled collection of buildings spanning several centuries. Joined to the land by a narrow, crumbling neck of rock, great cliffs protect this natural fortress on all sides, while a thick wall and a gatehouse protect the castle entrance.

The first castle to be built on this site was constructed in the 12th century, but virtually nothing remains of this early building. In the 14th century an L-plan tower house was built by William Keith, Marischal of Scotland. This building dominates the rest of the castle, its 50-foot (15m) walls still in good repair, although it is roofless. More buildings were raised in the 16th century, forming a handsome quadrangular courtyard. Although the emphasis was on comfort, rather than on defence, the castle was equipped with gun ports as a safeguard against possible attack. These were used twice in the 17th century during the Civil War, when the castle came under siege first by the Royalists, and then by Oliver Cromwell.

In a dark episode in the castle's history, it was used as a prison for 167 Scottish Presbyterians. These people were crammed into a long, narrow chamber known as the Whigs Vault, and conditions were so appalling that many of them died.

The weatherbeaten stones of Dunnottar Castle (left), in spectacular isolation above the North Sea (above)

DUNSKEY CASTLE Dumfries & Galloway

6 miles (10km) south west of Stranraer | **Exterior viewing only. Keep to the path** | **www.visitscotland.com**

Little is known of this ruined tower house standing on a rocky peninsula that juts out into the sea. A castle is mentioned in records dating to 1330, but was burned down early in the 15th century. A new tower was raised by William Adair of Kinhilt, but this was deserted in the middle of the 17th century and was little more than a ruin by 1684.

Dunskey is a simple L-plan tower house, with cellars, a ground floor and a first floor. Walls were built around the small peninsula, so that the castle would have been protected by two lines of defence: firstly the sea and ditches hewn from the rock, and secondly the castle walls. Virtually nothing remains of these walls, although there are still some traces of other buildings in what would have been the courtyard.

It is likely that Dunskey Castle would once have been a fine, proud fortified dwelling. The windows and doors were once decorated with dressed stones, but these, being expensive and much in demand for building, have been stripped away over the centuries by local looters. It is the absence of these stones that gives the roofless walls of Dunskey Castle their forlorn, rugged appearance. When viewing the castle you are advised to stay on the coastal path, as the surrounding cliffs are steep and dangerous.

Forlorn Dunskey Castle, stripped of its architectural riches, is perched on steep and dangerous cliffs

DUNTULM CASTLE Isle of Skye

This stronghold of the island clan of MacDonald stands in a commanding position overlooking a natural harbour at the extreme northern end of Skye. The rectangular tower dates from the 15th century, but a smaller tower was added in the 17th century, when the little fortress was at the height of its glory. Contemporary accounts tell of the lavish hospitality that could be enjoyed at the fine MacDonald house at Duntulm, and soil was imported from seven different countries to make the castle gardens fertile.

Several legends are attached to these atmospheric ruins. One is that the baby son of the clan chief was being dangled from a window by his nurse to see a passing ship when she inadvertently dropped him. The chief was reported to have quit Duntulm immediately before any further misfortunes should befall him.

A different tale involves another chief and his heir, Hugh. The story goes that Hugh was keen to inherit sooner rather than later, and so arranged for his kinsman's murder. In an act of appalling incompetence, Hugh misaddressed his letters, sending to the chief, not the invitation to dine, but instructions to the hired killer outlining how the foul deed was to be done. Hugh was arrested and immediately incarcerated in Duntulm's vaults with salt beef and nothing to drink. It is said that many years later a skeleton was unearthed, still pathetically clutching an empty water pitcher.

A fence surrounds the castle and anyone wishing to view the building is strongly recommended not to go beyond this boundary, as the castle is structurally unstable. There are long drops surrounding the ruin and parts of it have crumbled and fallen into the sea in recent years.

The precariously positioned ruins of Duntulm Castle should be viewed from a safe distance

DUNVEGAN CASTLE Isle of Skye

23 miles (37km) west of Portree | Open daily Apr to mid Oct, weekdays in winter (pre-arranged groups) | Tel: 01470 521206 | **www.dunvegancastle.com**

The story of Dunvegan Castle and its owners, the MacLeods, stretches back to the 13th century. In 1237 Leod, a son of the King of the Isle of Man and the North Isles, inherited the island of Lewis and Harris, and part of Skye. When Viking claims to the Scottish islands were finally crushed, Leod controlled a good portion of the Hebrides. He chose the rocky peninsula jutting out into the sea at Dunvegan on which to establish his fortress and headquarters. Dunvegan has remained the home of the MacLeods (meaning 'son of Leod') ever since. Leod died in 1280, but before his death a thick wall had been built around the site, leaving only a small sea gate, through which supplies could be brought to the castle in times of siege. Between 1340 and 1360, a keep was added, which contained kitchens and a dungeon. The Fairy

Tower was built around 1500, while further architectural improvements were made in the 17th century.

The entire castle was reconstructed in the 19th century, complete with noble battlements and little corner turrets, and today is an impressive sight, whether approached from land or sea. The gardens, originally laid out in the 18th century, are also quite magnificent.

One of Dunvegan's most curious treasures is the fabled 'Fairy Flag'. Modern tests have shown that this yellow silk banner dates from between AD 400 and AD 700 and comes from the Middle East, but how it came to be in the possession of the MacLeods is a mystery. There are many local legends about the flag: one story tells of how it was presented to a crusader MacLeod while he was in Palestine, while other legends insist that it was given to the family by fairies.

Above: Dunvegan's elegant drawing room
Left: The castle is one of Scotland's premier attractions

193

There was no capital city of Scotland, as such, until the end of the Middle Ages. Before that, Scotland's capital was wherever the king and his court happened to be. But the magnificent fortress squatting firmly on its plug of rock was a great favourite with Scottish kings, and has played a vital role in history on many occasions. It changed hands several times when the Scots were fighting for independence from England under Robert the Bruce, and became a royal residence under the Stuart kings.

Today, it is a museum – it houses the Scottish National War Memorial and the Scottish crown jewels – and is the world-renowned venue for the spectacular annual Edinburgh Military Tattoo in August. It still dominates the ancient city from its rocky pinnacle, and even though it has been battered and bruised throughout the centuries, it remains one of Britain's most impressive and best-known castles.

The origins of Edinburgh Castle are shrouded in mystery. Although the great rock on which the castle stands would probably have attracted earlier strongholds, there is no archaeological evidence to prove the site was used earlier than the 11th century. Malcolm III, before his death in 1093, raised a wooden fortress here, and his son, David I, built a church to the memory of his mother in the 1120s. This tiny chapel is the oldest surviving building in the castle. Thereafter, Edinburgh became an important gamepiece in the struggles between Edward I and Robert the Bruce in the late 13th century. Edward seized it in 1296, bombarding it with huge boulders from his great war machines. The garrison surrendered after only eight days, and Edward installed 350 of his own soldiers to hold it securely.

In 1313 the Earl of Moray, acting for Bruce, scaled the daunting cliffs with only 30 men and routed the English. Bruce then ordered

that the castle be utterly destroyed, so that it could never again be used by Edward's forces. He underestimated Edward's tenacity, for a few years later Edward retook the site, and set about repairing the damage, even planting gardens and orchards in anticipation of a lengthy stay. But the Scots were undeterred, and in 1341 a small party of soldiers disguised themselves as merchants and ambushed the startled garrison.

The vast sprawl of the castle contains buildings from many centuries. The fine half-moon battery and portcullis gate date from the 1570s, while the splendid Great Hall and the handsome palace were built for James IV in the early 16th century. In 1650, Cromwell bombarded the castle for three months, and in 1689 it came under heavy attack by the forces of William of Orange.

Above: The wood-panelled Great Hall
Left: The castle is perched high above the city
Right: The historic gatehouse is flanked by statues

EDZELL CASTLE Angus

8 miles (13km) north of Brechin | Open daily Apr to end Oct, Sat to Wed in winter | Tel: 01356 648631 | www.historic-scotland.gov.uk

The most remarkable feature of this sturdy little fortified tower house is its unusual gardens, complete with bath house and summer house. In 1604 a walled enclosure was added onto the already existing tower house and courtyard, designed to surround one of the most elegant and notable gardens of any castle in western Europe. The garden walls are a triumph in themselves: they have been divided into sections and are richly adorned with carvings and sculpted panels. Exquisite in their detail, the carvings embrace several themes: the first set depicts a number of planetary deities, including Mars, Jupiter, Venus and Saturn; the second represents the 'liberal arts'. In medieval learning, the three basic subjects were grammar, rhetoric and logic, while arithmetic, music, geometry and astronomy were the four more advanced topics. Each of these seven subjects is illustrated by seated figures busily practising their art.

The tower house was built in the 15th century as a home for the Lindsay family. Other buildings, arranged around a courtyard, were added in the 16th century. Edzell saw little military action, although it was occupied by Oliver Cromwell's Parliamentarian troops in 1651, and was badly damaged in the second Jacobite uprising in 1747. Today, the tower remains the most complete section, along with the quaint summer house in the south-east corner of the garden.

Left and below: The garden walls at Edzell Castle, most of which remain today, are highly decorated

EILEAN DONAN CASTLE Highland

8 miles (13km) east of Kyle of Lochalsh | Open daily Mar to end Oct | Tel: 01599 555202 | www.eileandonancastle.com

Dwarfed by the brooding hills surrounding Loch Duich, the castle of Eilean Donan stands picturesquely on its rocky island, at the point where three great sea lochs meet. A fortress was built here in 1220 by Alexander II to protect himself against raids by Vikings. During the Jacobite uprising the Macraes opted to support the Old Pretender and garrisoned a small force of Spanish soldiers in the castle. In 1719 the guns of an English man-of-war pounded the castle to pieces. It remained in ruins until 1912, when Colonel John Macrae decided to restore his ancestral home. Paying great attention to detail, the lakeside castle was lovingly rebuilt, along with an arched bridge that affords easier access to the castle than the ancient Macraes would have known.

Most of the rooms in the castle are open to visitors, all furnished in the style of the home of a country laird. There are fine collections of pistols and powder horns, and, although it is mostly a 20th-century restoration, it allows the imagination to return to the time when the castle was owned by the wild Macraes. A fearsome clan, they relished displaying the heads of their enemies on the battlements, and local legends tell how, on one occasion, they defended the castle successfully when outnumbered by their attackers 400 to one.

Above left: The bloodthirsty Macraes once displayed the heads of their enemies on these battlements

Above and overleaf: The castle today in its peaceful setting on the picturesque lakeside

FLOORS CASTLE Border

🦁 1 mile (1.6km) north west of Kelso | Open selected days throughout the year | Tel: 01573 223333 | www.roxburghe.net

The family home of the Innes Kers, Floors has been described as the largest inhabited castle in Britain. It started its existence as a large house, built between 1718 and 1740 for the 1st Duke of Roxburghe, John Ker. Until recently it was believed that Sir John Vanbrugh had drawn up the plans, but it is now known to be the work of William Adam.

On the 1st Duke's death in 1740, Floors quickly passed through his son Robert to John, the 3rd Duke, in 1755. The death of his heir, an elderly cousin, in the following year sparked off a celebrated crisis – the Roxburghe Peerage Case – with a number of distant relatives eagerly claiming the title. The matter was finally decided in 1812 by the Committee of Privileges of the House of Lords, who came down in favour of Sir James

Innes. Taking the title 5th Duke and the name Innes Ker, Sir James was forced to sell his predecessor's famous library to cover the costs of his claim.

The 6th Duke, James, was to further the family fortunes through his connections at court, earning himself a peerage and a state visit from Queen Victoria in 1867 – a summerhouse in the garden was built especially for her. The 6th Duke was also responsible for changing the face of Floors, engaging the great William Playfair, noted for his work in Edinburgh New Town, to remodel and extend the house.

Playfair added a delightful roofscape of lead cupolas more reminiscent of French than Scottish architectural traditions to Floors Castle, as well as features ranging from the

Magnificent Floors Castle was built in the grand style

Grand Ballroom to a Gothic-style chamber specifically built to hold the Duke's collection of stuffed birds.

While the outside of Floors has barely changed since that time, extensive remodelling of the interior was undertaken during the era of the 8th Duke, Sir Henry Innes Ker, who inherited it in 1892. In 1903 the 8th Duke married American heiress Mary Goelet. Her greatest contribution is probably the collection of antique tapestries, many brought from her Long Island home. Duchess May, as she was known, also acquired paintings by Matisse and ornaments by Fabergé. Together they form one of the chief attractions of Floors today.

200

GLAMIS CASTLE Angus

🦁 **12 miles (19km) north of Dundee** | **Open daily Apr to end Dec** | **Tel: 01307 840393** | **www.glamis-castle.co.uk**

Legends and myths about Glamis Castle are plentiful. It was used as a setting in Shakespeare's *Macbeth* (although this was historically inaccurate); Malcolm II was said to have been murdered here in the 11th century; Lady Janet Douglas, the widow of the Earl of Glamis, was burned at the stake as a witch here by James V in 1540; and there is said to be a secret room where one lord of Glamis played cards with the devil. It is difficult to associate such dark tales with this splendidly ornate, dark red castle.

There was probably a castle at Glamis in the early 14th century, but it was not until after 1376 that the L-plan tower house was built by John Lyon on land presented to him by King Robert II. The Lyon family, now Earls of Strathmore and Kinghorne, have owned the castle ever since.

If Glamis today looks more like a French chateau than a medieval fortress, it is because the castle was extensively restored and developed in the 17th and 18th centuries. The original tower house, although strengthened, heightened and re-roofed, remains the central part of this rambling palace. Tours of the house range from the medieval hall to the 17th-century chapel, and include the small suite of rooms used by George VI and Queen Elizabeth The Queen Mother, who lived here as a child.

Previous page: The elegant entrance to Glamis Castle
Above: The castle surrounded by snow in winter
Below left: The dining room set for a private dinner
Below: Elizabeth The Queen Mother's bedroom

HERMITAGE CASTLE Border

15 miles (24km) south of Hawick | Open daily Apr to end Sep | Tel: 01387 376222 | www.historic-scotland.gov.uk

Hermitage Castle's impregnable-looking sandstone walls loom menacingly across the Borders, and Sir Walter Scott recorded that local people regarded this brooding fortress 'with peculiar aversion and terror'.

The merest glance explains why, for the walls rise sheer and imposing from among the grassy earthworks, and windows are few and far between. The only significant openings are the rows of doors on the very top part of the castle, which afforded access to the wooden fighting balcony that once protruded from the walls. The Douglas family developed the tower from a simple 13th-century rectangular building to the grim, late 14th-century fortress that can be seen today.

One of the two great flying arches was reconstructed in the 19th century, but, all in all, Hermitage today appears much as it would have done in the 15th century.

Several of Hermitage's owners committed foul deeds within its walls. One drowned a colleague near the castle, but was later boiled alive for his misdeeds, which included witchcraft. Another starved his enemies to death in the pit dungeons, although he too met an unpleasant end, murdered in a nearby forest. And Hermitage Castle was also the place where Mary, Queen of Scots rushed to be at the bedside of her ailing lover, the Earl of Bothwell.

The river that runs near the castle is known as Hermitage Water. And some 600 feet (180m) away from the castle, on the banks of the river, stand the remains of the medieval hermitage that gave Hermitage Castle its name.

The castle stands on a hillock near Hermitage Water

HUNTLY CASTLE Aberdeenshire

This once magnificent, palatial castle is now decayed and crumbling, but has nonetheless been described as one of the noblest baronial ruins in Scotland. Approaching the castle along the avenue of trees, you are faced with the vast five-storeyed facade, with its inscriptions, fine oriel windows and handsome carvings. A former Catholic stronghold, Huntly Castle remains an elegant and imposing ruin, set in the delightful green countryside of Aberdeenshire.

There have been three castles at Huntly. In the 12th century a mound and wooden structure were raised by the Normans, and Robert the Bruce stayed here in 1307, but this building was burned down. In the early 15th century, the Gordons built a second castle, of which only the foundations remain.

However, in the 1450s the 4th Earl of Huntly began what he called his 'new werk' and this was the basis of the palatial castle that can be seen today. Although it was intended to be an elegant residence, defence was not totally abandoned in favour of comfort. The walls are thick, and there are gun ports and iron gates for added protection.

In 1594 the 5th Earl revolted against King James VI, who then attacked Huntly with gunpowder. Royal favour was lost and won quickly, however; three years later the castle was restored to the Earl, and building resumed. In 1640 Huntly was occupied by the Covenanters, a religious and political group.

Carvings above a doorway of the ruin (below) show the coat of arms of George Gordon and King James VI (left)

INNIS CHONNEL CASTLE Argyll & Bute

18 miles (29km) east of Oban | Exterior viewing only | www.scotlandsplaces.gov.uk

In the 15th century, Donald, infant heir to the Lord of the Isles, was brought to the island fortress of Innis Chonnel as a prisoner by the Campbell clan. By the time he managed to escape, Donald had reached adulthood. He did not enjoy his freedom for long, for he was recaptured after an ill-conceived invasion of Badenoch in 1503 and taken to Edinburgh, where he remained a prisoner for 40 years.

Innis Chonnel was an important stronghold of the Campbells of Argyll and was one of their earliest castles. Local tradition suggests that the castle dates from the 11th century, along with the founders of the great Campbell clan, although there is no architectural evidence that it is so old.

The present building, a squat, square tower, draped in ivy and nestling amid trees, probably dates from the 13th century and was enlarged in the 15th century. The alterations changed the castle from a simple rectangular tower to a strong enclosure

Innis Chonnel Castle in the evening light. This early Campbell stronghold is thought to be 700 years old

with thick walls following the shape of the island, complete with additional towers. Innis Chonnel still occupies its little island in Loch Awe, although the view of the castle from the road is somewhat obscured by trees, especially in summer.

The island is privately owned and there is no public access.

INVERARAY CASTLE
Argyll & Bute

Just north of Inveraray | Open daily Apr to Oct | Tel: 01499 302203 | www.inveraray-castle.com

The history of Clan Campbell dates back to 1266 and beyond, and could fill volumes, but the senior branch of the family, the Earls of Argyll, moved into a fortified tower with a small settlement nearby, at the mouth of the River Aray, in the 15th century.

The dukedom was conferred on the 10th Earl by a grateful William of Orange in 1701; by 1720 the 2nd Duke, a great Hanoverian soldier, was thinking of remodelling the castle to designs by Sir John Vanbrugh – but it was his brother Archibald, succeeding him in 1743, who threw himself into the task.

Most of what can be seen at Inveraray today was planned by the 3rd Duke, including the township, the castle and the beautiful surrounding parkland. The foundation stone was laid in 1746, just yards away from the old tower (which was not demolished until 1773). The basic square structure, including the central tower, was completed by 1758 to a design by Roger Morris. One of the most appealing features of the estate was also built at this time: the watchtower high on Duniquaich was constructed in 1748, for £46.

There is a great sense of space and light in the State Dining Room, which was created from one end of the Long Gallery when a modest entrance hall was built in the middle in 1772. The elaborate wall paintings of flower garlands and fruit, with little animals, faces, peacock feathers and so on, are encased in finely gilded panels. With the central friezes, the decoration is in the French style made popular by the young Prince of Wales at Carlton House, yet this is the only work to survive by the two French artists Girard and Guinard. The quality of the painting here and in the drawing room is unique and exquisite, enhanced by the pretty French tapestry work on the gilded furniture.

The Tapestry Drawing Room is hung with beautiful Beauvais tapestries, commissioned by the 5th Duke, with further painting on a delicate ceiling by Robert Adam. The floral-themed room is dominated by a lovely portrait by Hoppner of the 5th Duke's daughter, Lady Charlotte, as 'Flora'.

Below: The castle surrounded by stunning parkland
Right: Wall-mounted weapons in the Armoury Hall

KILCHURN CASTLE Argyll & Bute

18 miles (29km) east of Oban | Open daily Apr to Sep | Tel: 0131 668 8081 | www.historic-scotland.gov.uk

In an area of reeds and marshes at the northern end of Loch Awe stands ruined Kilchurn Castle, its granite walls and chimneys rising like jagged teeth above the trees. Its position on a peninsula reaching out into the loch gave it some protection from attack on three sides.

The beauty of Kilchurn's setting on this lovely loch has attracted many an artist, but on closer inspection, time has not dealt kindly with the little lakeside fortress and only a shell remains to be seen. Until recently, Kilchurn's unstable walls were a danger to visitors, but these have been secured and the castle may now be viewed from the grounds.

Kilchurn Castle began as a simple square tower with five floors. It was raised in the 15th century by Colin Campbell, 1st Earl of Breadalbane. In the 16th and 17th centuries, the castle was extended. The square tower was incorporated into a small courtyard, with three corner towers, forming an irregular quadrangle. Oddly, the only way into the castle seems to have been through the main door of the keep and across its ground floor. Gun loops placed at regular intervals all around the walls suggest that Kilchurn's builders were more concerned with repelling sudden attacks by Highlanders than with resisting lengthy sieges.

Below left: Kilchurn Castle was built to resist sudden attacks from marauding Highlanders

Below left: Kilchurn Castle was built to resist sudden attacks from marauding Highlanders

Below: The waters of Loch Awe reflect Kilchurn Castle surrounded by breathtaking autumnal colours

KILDRUMMY CASTLE Aberdeenshire

15 miles (24km) south of Huntly | Open daily Apr to end Sep | Tel: 01975 571331 | **www.historic-scotland.gov.uk**

Robert the Bruce was married twice. His first wife was a daughter of the powerful Earl of Mar and his second was from the English de Burgh family. Through his first marriage, Robert came into possession of Kildrummy Castle, and it figured prominently in the Scottish Wars of Independence against Edward I of England.

Like Stirling and Bothwell castles, Kildrummy changed hands several times, most notably after the siege of 1306. Robert's brother, Nigel, had been left in charge of Kildrummy while other supporters of the defeated Bruce hurried north, away from Edward's advancing troops. When Edward laid siege to Kildrummy, Nigel withstood every assault, and his constant counter-attacks made life in the siege camp unbearable. The castle finally fell because of Osbourne, a treacherous blacksmith who was offered gold in return for setting Kildrummy on fire. The garrison surrendered, and Nigel was later executed at Berwick.

Kildrummy Castle today is a seven-sided enclosure with two round towers, two D-shaped towers and a sturdy gatehouse, very much like the one at Harlech. Today, most of this once mighty fortress exists only as foundations in the grass, although some of the towers have survived to first-floor level.

The Elphinstone Tower, built by the family of the same name (left), and the outer north-eastern facade (below), with the central chapel and Warden's Tower

LINLITHGOW PALACE West Lothian

7 miles (11km) south of Grangemouth | **Open daily all year** | **Tel: 01506 842896** | **www.historic-scotland.gov.uk**

Rising dramatically from the shores of Linlithgow Loch is a great square palace-fortress, which dates from the 15th century. Although there was a fortified residence here as early as the mid-12th century, and Edward I built a manor here in 1302, it was not until 1425 that work began on the castle that may be seen today.

King James I of Scotland gave orders that a royal residence should be constructed on the site of the earlier buildings, and although Linlithgow was primarily a palace, the architect incorporated a number of defensive features. There was a drawbridge and a barbican, and the walls of the four corner towers were immensely thick. The windows in the lower floors were protected by iron bars, the holes for which can still be seen in the stone. Around the early 1500s, machicolations were added.

Linlithgow has played its part in Scotland's history. Mary, Queen of Scots was born here in 1542, Charles I slept here in 1633 and Oliver Cromwell stayed in the palace in the winter of 1650–51. When the Duke of Cumberland's army bivouacked in Linlithgow in 1746 en route to their encounter with Prince Charles Edward Stuart's army at Culloden Moor, fires were left burning which gutted this handsome building.

Right: The square fortress seen from its courtyard
Below: Engraving of Linlithgow published in 1830

LOCH LEVEN CASTLE Perth & Kinross

10 miles (16km) north of Dunfermline | Open daily Apr to end Oct | Tel: 01577 862670 | www.historic-scotland.gov.uk

The only way to reach the ancient fortress of Loch Leven is by boat, even though the waters of the loch today are lower than they were in the 14th century when the castle was built. This is because the course of the River Leven was altered in the 19th century, and the level of the loch was lowered as a result. The castle itself is a simple square tower of five storeys, surrounded by a towered wall that was a later addition. The third floor of the tower was possibly where Mary, Queen of Scots was imprisoned between June 1567 and May 1568. There are also the remains of what may have been a private chapel, complete with an altar shelf containing a basin, and a small wall cupboard. In another window is a closet that may have been used as a strong room in which to store valuables.

Queen Mary was unwell for much of the time she was imprisoned at Loch Leven, and she suffered a miscarriage. She escaped from the castle by befriending the boat keeper, but after the Battle of Langside, during which Mary and her supporters were soundly defeated, she fled the country.

Aspects of dramatically situated Loch Leven Castle (left and above), which is accessible only by boat (top left)

NEIDPATH CASTLE Border

After Scotland had won her independence from England in the 14th century under great warriors like William Wallace and Robert the Bruce, local landowners had the task of establishing law and order in their domains. Castles such as the one at Neidpath were built, not only to provide a form of defence, should the laird come under attack, but also so that he could maintain a tighter control over his subjects.

Neidpath's L-plan tower was built in the second half of the 14th century, and the upper two floors were remodelled in the 17th century. The tower is unusual because both arms of the L form parallelograms rather than rectangles, as was most common, and the corners are rounded. It is an intriguing building, its four main floors intersected with mural passages and 'entresols', or mezzanine floors, giving the impression that the castle is full of small chambers and passages, all at different heights.

The lower floor contained a pit prison and a well, while on the second floor is a room with some fine 17th-century panelling.

Mary, Queen of Scots and James I and VI stayed at Neidpath, although the castle has been too much altered since the 16th century for it to be possible to identify which rooms they occupied.

Previous page: This view of the castle from the River Tweed has barely changed over the centuries
Above: Up close, the castle is badly damaged
Right: Attractive stonework on the entrance gateway into the castle courtyard

ORCHARDTON TOWER Dumfries & Galloway

4½ miles (7km) south of Dalbeattie | Open access all year | Tel: 0131 668 8081 (office hours) | www.historic-scotland.gov.uk

Of all the small tower houses and castles built in 15th-century Scotland, Orchardton is the one that gives the visitor a clear impression of what domestic life must have been like in Scottish medieval feudal society. The rooms inside the tower are small, cramped and dark, with narrow windows, which perhaps would have made for warmer living quarters – they certainly would have made the tower more secure from attack. But during winter, with the shutters firmly closed against the cold and a smoking fire in the hearth, Orchardton Castle would not have been a cheerful dwelling.

Orchardton is unusual in being the only round tower house in Scotland, and since it was built in the mid-15th century by the family of the Provost of Lincluden, Alexander Cairns, it has had many different uses.

The basement had a vaulted roof, and, unlike the other floors, is rectangular. The narrow spiral staircase is in the thickness of the wall, and rises to the top of the 33-foot (10m) high tower, where there is a gabled watchtower. As in Norman keeps, the entrance was on the first floor, so that the wooden steps which gave access to the tower could be drawn up inside the building during times of danger.

Orchardton Tower, the only round tower in Scotland (right), dwarfed by the bulk of Screel Hill (below)

ST ANDREWS CASTLE Fife

🦁 **13 miles (21km) south east of Dundee | Open daily all year | Tel: 01334 477196 | www.historic-scotland.gov.uk**

In March 1546 the Protestant preacher George Wishart was burned in front of the walls of St Andrews Castle by the ambitious Archbishop of St Andrews, Cardinal David Beaton. Beaton was not a popular man, chiefly because he refused to agree to the marriage of Henry VIII's Protestant son to the Scottish King's Catholic daughter. Later that year, a group of Protestant Fife lairds gained access to the castle and murdered Beaton, hanging his body from the castle walls in a pair of sheets. Following this, a long siege began, as the forces of the Regent of Scotland tried to oust them from the castle.

It was during this turbulent time that the famous mine and countermine were dug. The attackers' mine was intended to go underneath the foundations, so that the wall would weaken, while the countermine attempted to stop it. You can still walk through these two tunnels, which give a unique insight into medieval warfare.

This ancient castle was built and used by the bishops and archbishops of St Andrews. It comprises a five-sided enclosure, protected on two sides by the sea, with buildings dating from the 12th to the 16th centuries that served as palace, fortress and prison. One of the castle's most famous features is its sinister bottle dungeon. This is a pit 24 feet (7.3m) deep, which is narrow at the top and wider at the bottom – much like the shape of a bottle. Once you are inside, you cannot scale the walls to escape. Hewn out of solid rock, it has no windows or openings for air.

The ruined shell of St Andrews Castle (right) is spread over a spectacular coastal location (below and far right)

STIRLING CASTLE Stirling

In Stirling city centre | Open daily all year | Tel: 01786 450000 | www.stirlingcastle.gov.uk

Perched high and proud on its towering cliffs, Stirling Castle is a complex arrangement of buildings – some plain and functional, others splendid and palatial – that reflect its long history as one of the most important castles in Scotland.

Most of the buildings that can be seen today date from the 15th century or later, and it is not known exactly what the castle was like before this, when it was being fought over by William Wallace, Robert the Bruce and Edward I. This eventful history began in the late 11th century, when a wooden structure was raised. Edward I seized Stirling in 1296 and Wallace took it back in 1297. He lost it again in 1298, but the Scots reclaimed it once more in 1299. Edward retrieved the castle after a furious siege in 1304, and this time held it until the English defeat at Bannockburn in 1314.

There are many fine buildings to explore in this splendid fortress. Perhaps the most impressive is the Great Hall, which is one of the earliest Renaissance buildings in Scotland and also by far the largest banqueting hall in the country. The elegant palace was built for James V in the 1540s, and there are some exquisite carvings, both inside (around the fireplaces) and on the exterior walls. Other highlights include the great kitchens, the chapel royal and Argyll's Lodging – a splendid example of a 17th-century Scottish townhouse, situated on the upper approaches to the castle and built for a nobleman serving the royal court. Also of interest is the Regimental Museum, where you can see exhibits and memorabilia associated with the Argyll and Sutherland Highlanders regiment, and the Tapestry Studio, where you can watch weavers at work, recreating seven medieval tapestries to hang on the walls of the Queen's Inner Hall within the palace.

Wooden roof trusses in the Great Hall (right), one of the highlights of a visit to magnificent Stirling Castle (top)

TANTALLON CASTLE East Lothian

2½ miles (4km) east of North Berwick | Open daily Apr to end Oct, Sat to Wed in winter | Tel: 01620 892727 | www.historic-scotland.gov.uk

The great red walls of Tantallon Castle form one of the strongest and most daunting castles in Scotland. Perched on a spur of rock, with sheer cliffs plummeting into frothing seas on three of its sides, the fourth side is protected by a formidable array of ditches and walls. Rising from one of the three great gaping ditches, and sweeping clear across the neck of the promontory, is a vast curtain of red sandstone. This wall is 12 feet (3.7m) thick, and a staggering 50 feet (15m) tall. Although cannons and storms have battered this mighty wall, it remains one of the most impressive defensive features of any castle in Britain.

Tantallon is associated with one of Scotland's most famous families – the Red Douglases, Earls of Angus. It came into their hands at the end of the 14th century, and became their base as they plotted and fought against their enemies. But it was not until 1528 that the mighty fortress of Tantallon was put to the test, when King James V himself laid siege to the Red Douglas stronghold.

Sixteenth-century Scottish politics were complicated, but, essentially, Archibald Douglas, 6th Earl of Angus, had kept the young James V a virtual prisoner in Edinburgh during his minority. James finally managed to escape, and once he was old enough to act for himself, he charged Douglas with treason. James brought a great battery of guns from

Dunbar Castle, and for 20 days pounded the walls of Tantallon with everything he had. Tantallon, however, stood firm – perhaps because the great ditches to the front of the castle prevented the guns from being brought too close, and perhaps because the King ran short of powder and shot. The castle eventually fell to James, but as a result of negotiations rather than firepower. Douglas fled the country, and James began work to reinforce and repair Tantallon's medieval defences. After the King's death, Douglas returned from exile in 1543 and immediately began plotting against the Regent of Scotland, the Earl of Arran.

The ruins at Tantallon are impressive, and the Mid Tower, which has been changed and developed through the centuries, stands almost complete. It was originally five storeys, but suffered during the 1528 siege. In 1556, a Fore Tower was added, designed both to withstand and to house cannons. The East Tower was also five storeys, and there are still stairs in the massive curtain wall that lead to the battlements. To withstand sieges, arrangements were made for the castle to

take in supplies from the seaward side. The remains of a crane bastion can be seen, where provisions were winched from boats anchored below, and it is likely that there was another one in the now ruined sea gate.

There are stunning views of the sea-bird colony on the Bass Rock (above) from the formidable curtain wall of Tantallon Castle (top). An early engraving shows the castle at the mercy of stormy seas (left)

TOLQUHON CASTLE Aberdeenshire

'All this warke excep the auld tour was begun be William Forbes 15 Aprile 1584 and endit be him 20 October 1589.' These words are inscribed in a panel high up on the right-hand side of the imposing gatehouse at Tolquhon Castle (pronounced 'Tuh-hon'). They refer to the work of the 7th Lord of Tolquhon, the cultured William Forbes, who inherited the castle in the late 16th century. Before Tolquhon came into Forbes' possession, it was little more than a single tower (the 'auld tour') with some adjoining walls. But in 1584, Forbes decided the tower was insufficient for his needs, and set about extending it. The result was the fine palatial building that can be visited today, and although Tolquhon is now a ruin, it takes little imagination to envisage how splendid this castle must have looked in its heyday.

The 'auld tour', or Preston's Tower, was raised in the early 15th century, probably by John Preston, its namesake. It was built of granite, with thick walls, and had small rooms, which would have been ill-lit and probably cramped for the people living in them. Little remains of Preston's Tower except the vaulted basement and parts of the first floor. Forbes used it as one of the corners of his new castle, and extended the building to make a four-sided structure around a large courtyard. The castle was entered through a gatehouse which, although it appears to be formidable with its gun loops and round towers, had thin walls and would not have withstood a serious attack. It was designed for show, rather than defence.

An impressive array of buildings line all four sides of the fine cobbled courtyard. To the east are the kitchens and an unpleasant pit prison, while the main house is to the south. This building contained the hall – a spacious, airy room lit by large windows – and the laird's personal chambers, along with additional bed chambers and a gallery. Contemporary records show that William Forbes owned many books, and it is likely that they would have been displayed here.

Forbes' renovations did not stop with his fine new house. The hall and his private chamber looked out over a formal garden, and though this has long since disappeared, the remains of a dovecote and recesses for bees have been discovered in the walls.

The ruins of Tolquhon Castle (above) are entered through a sturdy-looking gatehouse (left)

URQUHART CASTLE Moray

16 miles (26km) south west of Inverness | Open daily all year | Tel: 01456 450551 | www.historic-scotland.gov.uk

In 1545 the fearsome MacDonald clan swept into the quiet Glen of Urquhart, looting and pillaging as they went. They laid siege to the castle and plundered it mercilessly, taking chairs, tables, gates, armour, food and even the pillows from the beds. After the castle had been thoroughly sacked, the raiders turned their attention to the homesteads in the valley. This was just one incident in a long history of warfare and bloodshed that had raged since a castle was first built on the shores of Loch Ness in the early 13th century. The first recorded owner of the castle was Alan Durward, Lord of Atholl. Durward's brother-in-law was Alexander II, King of Scotland, and it would seem that the young King was very much under the influence of his powerful relative.

In 1296 Edward I of England seized Urquhart along with other castles in the area, but his hold was precarious and he lost it again by 1303. Edward marched north and retook the castle, but within five years Robert the Bruce had attacked Edward's garrison and secured Urquhart for himself.

Although Urquhart remained in the hands of the Scottish government during the 14th and 15th centuries, it was not an easy ownership. Not only was the castle under threat from the English, but there was a constant threat from the Lords of the Isles. These fiercely independent people had been forced into the Kingdom of Scotland after the Battle of Largs in 1263, and were so keen to regain their freedom that they even sided with the English. Urquhart passed from the Lords of the Isles to the Scottish government and back again in a series of bloody encounters that continued until the Lordship of the Isles no longer existed.

In view of its turbulent history, it is not surprising that Urquhart's defences are formidable. A walled causeway, with a drawbridge halfway along, led to the castle gatehouse. Great walls that followed the contours of the rock protected it from attack, strengthened by a ditch at the front and the loch at the back. Inside the walls were a variety of buildings, including living quarters, a chapel, kitchens and a dovecote.

Although much of the building is dilapidated, apart from the 16th-century tower house, which is still largely intact, this romantic ruin huddled on the loch shore in Drumnadrochit is well worth a visit. It is also the site from where many people claim to have spotted the Loch Ness Monster, and webcams (live footage of which can be seen on the internet) are set up above the castle just in case 'Nessie' should make an appearance in the loch.

Urquhart Castle on the romantic shores of Loch Ness

ACKNOWLEDGEMENTS

The Automobile Association wishes to thank the following photographers, companies and picture libraries for their assistance in the preparation of this book. Abbreviations are as follows – (t) top; (b) bottom; (l) left; (r) right; (c) centre; (AA) AA World Travel Library.

2/3 AA/L Noble; 6 AA; 7tl Last Refuge/Alamy; 7tr Skyscan Photolibrary/Alamy; 7cl Adrian Sherratt/Alamy; 7cr David Burton/Alamy; 7bl david speight/Alamy; 7br AA/N Setchfield; 8 Parrott Images/Alamy; 9 Jon Arnold Images Ltd/Alamy; 10 The National Trust Photolibrary/Alamy; 11l AA/D Hall; 11c The National Trust Photolibrary/Alamy; 11r Nigel Hicks/Alamy; 12l AA/D Hall; 12r AA/D Hall; 13 AA/D Hall; 14/15 AA/A Burton; 15 AA/A Newey; 16 Pat Eyre/Alamy; 17 Stuart Black/Alamy; 18t The National Trust Photolibrary/Alamy; 18b The National Trust Photolibrary/Alamy; 19 AA/R Moss; 20 David Hansford/Alamy; 21l Cameni Images/Alamy; 21r Robin Weaver/Alamy; 22t Powderham Castle; 22b Powderham Castle; 23 Powderham Castle; 24t David Chapman/Alamy; 24b James Handfield-Jones/Alamy; 25t AA/C Jones; 25b The National Trust Photolibrary/Alamy; 26t Sherborne Castle; 26b Sherborne Castle; 27 © Xander Casey; 28 AA/J Wood; 29 Image Source/Alamy; 30 AA/M Busselle; 31l AA/S Montgomery; 31cr Greg Balfour Evans/Alamy; 31br AA/L Noble; 32 Last Refuge/Robert Harding; 33t AA/L Noble; 33b AA/L Noble; 34/35 AA/L Noble; 36t Last Refuge/Alamy; 36b The National Trust Photolibrary/Alamy; 37 AA/L Noble; 38 AA/A Burton; 39t David Pressland/Alamy; 39b Available Light Photography/Alamy; 40t Martin Briggs; 40b Martin Briggs; 41 nobleIMAGES/Alamy; 42/43 AA/N Setchfield; 43 Jon Arnold Images Ltd/Alamy; 44/45 AA/S & O Mathews; 45 Angelo Hornak/Alamy; 46 AA/D Forss; 47 Hever Castle Ltd; 48 AA/L Noble; 49t AA/L Noble; 49b AA/L Noble; 50l Manor Photography/Alamy; 50r AA ; 51t AA/A Newey; 51b AA/A Newey; 52 AA/N Setchfield; 53t Ian Goodrick/Alamy; 53bl Peter Staniforth/Alamy; 53br Peter Staniforth/Alamy; 54 AA/S Montgomery; 55t AA/S Montgomery; 55b AA/S Montgomery; 56t AA/J Tims; 56b AA/J Tims; 57 AA/J Tims; 58 AA/I Burgum; 59l Manor Photography/Alamy; 59c AA/I Burgum; 59r mark saunders/Alamy; 60 Rolf Richardson/Alamy; 61t Mike Hayward/Alamy; 61b Mike Hayward/Alamy; 62t AA/G Matthews; 62b Chris Howes/Wild Places Photography/Alamy; 62/63 The Photolibrary Wales/Alamy; 64l AA/M Bauer; 64r AA/R Newton; 64/65 AA/M Bauer; 66 AA/R Duke; 67 AA/I Burgum; 68t AA/R Duke; 68b AA/R Duke; 69 AA/R Duke; 70t AA/C Warren; 70b AA/C Warren; 71t AA/H Williams; 71bl AA/R Duke; 71br AA/I Burgum; 72 Lee Pengelly/Alamy; 73t AA/R Duke; 73b Michael Hudson/Alamy; 74t The National Trust Photolibrary/Alamy; 74b AA/N Jenkins; 75 AA/M Bauer; 76 Tony Cox/Alamy; 76/77 Alan Novelli/Alamy; 78l Liquid Light/Alamy; 78r The Photolibrary Wales/Alamy; 79t AA/M Bauer; 79b AA/M Bauer; 80 David Noton Photography/Alamy; 81t AA/P Aithie; 81b Dave Henrys/Alamy; 82t AA/H Williams; 82b AA/H Williams; 83l AA/G Mathews; 83r Alan King Etching 07/Alamy; 84 AA/M Bauer; 84/85 AA/M Bauer; 86/87 architecture UK/Alamy; 87t Steve Atkins Photography/Alamy; 87b iWebbtravel/Alamy; 88t Adrian Sherratt/Alamy; 88bl AA/J Gravell; 88br Chris Howes/Wild Places Photography/Alamy; 89t Liquid Light/Alamy; 89b Robert Evans/Alamy; 90 AA/C Jones; 91 Stephen Dorey/Alamy; 92 Manor Photography/Alamy; 93 AA/J Gravell; 92/93 CW Images/Alamy; 94t Jeremy Hoare/Alamy; 94b Camera Lucida/Alamy; 95 The National Trust Photolibrary/Alamy; 96 The National Trust Photolibrary/Alamy; 97 The National Trust Photolibrary/Alamy; 98t Angelo Hornak/Alamy; 98b Chris Howes/Wild Places Photography/Alamy; 99t james jagger/Alamy; 99b Christine Strover/Alamy; 100l Chris Howes/Wild Places Photography/Alamy; 100r AA/D Santillo; 101t Jeff Morgan 03/Alamy; 101b Jeff Morgan 05/Alamy; 102 Tom Mackie/Alamy; 103l Glyn Thomas/Alamy; 103c david willats/Alamy; 103r The National Trust Photolibrary/Alamy; 104l Tracey Whitefoot/Alamy; 104r jaxpix/Alamy; 105t David Burton/Alamy; 105b John Worrall/Alamy; 106t Last Refuge/Alamy; 106b Martin Beddall/Alamy; 107 AA/R J Edwards; 108t AA/R Surman; 108b geodigital/Alamy; 109 AA/C Jones; 110 AA/D Forss; 111tl David Cantrille/Alamy; 111tr david willats/Alamy; 111b Robin Weaver/Alamy; 112 AA/C Jones; 113l Sue Heaton/Alamy; 113tr AA/I Burgum; 113cr Jeff Morgan 06/Alamy; 114 AA/N Setchfield; 115t World History Archive/Alamy; 115b Skyscan Photolibrary/Alamy; 116 AA/H Palmer; 116/117 AA/C Jones; 118 Mike Kipling Photography/Alamy; 119l AA/T Mackie; 119r geodigital/Alamy; 120 Rockingham Castle; 121 Tony Pleavin/photolibrary.com; 122 AA; 123t The National Trust Photolibrary/Alamy; 123bl The National Trust Photolibrary/Alamy; 123br The National Trust Photolibrary/Alamy; 124 Antony Nettle/Alamy; 125l CJG-UK/Alamy; 125r Chris Cooper-Smith/Alamy; 126/127 AA/C Jones; 128 AA/J Hunt; 129tl AA/J Hunt; 129bl Stephen Bradley/Alamy; 129r Holmes Garden Photos/Alamy; 130t AA/T Woodcock; 130b AA/J Hunt; 131 AA/C Lees; 132 AA/J Hunt; 132/133 AA/J Hunt; 134t AA/G Rowatt; 134b AA/C Lees; 135t brinkstock/Alamy; 135b Simon Whaley/Alamy; 136t AA/J Morrison; 136b Ros Drinkwater/Alamy; 137 Stephen Meese/Alamy; 138t Parrott Images/Alamy; 138b julie woodhouse/Alamy; 139 AA/R Coulam; 140t Holmes Garden Photos/Alamy; 140b Ashley Cooper/Alamy; 141 AA/R Coulam; 142 Chipchase Castle; 143l AA/R Newton; 143r Mark Sunderland/Alamy; 144 AA/J Hunt; 145l Paul Melling/Alamy; 145r curved-light/Alamy; 146 AA/J Hunt; 147t The National Trust Photolibrary/Alamy; 147bl AA/J Hunt; 147br The National Trust Photolibrary/Alamy; 148/149 AA/J Hunt; 150 Steve Bishop; 151t Andrew Michael/Alamy; 151b Clearview/Alamy; 152t Troy GB images/Alamy; 152bl Troy GB images/Alamy; 152br Mary Evans Picture Library/Alamy; 153 Britain on View/photolibrary.com; 154t Holmes Garden Photos/Alamy; 154b Trinity Mirror/Mirrorpix/Alamy; 155t AA; 155b Raby Castle, Raby Estates; 156/157 ICP/Alamy; 157t AA/P Baker; 157b David Bagley/Alamy; 158 Ripley Castle; 159l 19th era/Alamy; 159r AA/P Baker; 160 The National Trust Photolibrary/Alamy; 161 The National Trust Photolibrary/Alamy; 162l AA/T Mackie; 162r AA/L Whitwam; 163 AA/J Hunt; 165l Collpicto/Alamy; 165c David Robertson/Alamy; 165r David Kilpatrick/Alamy; 166 pictureproject/Alamy; 167 David Lyons/Alamy; 168 Ayton Castle; 169 Ayton Castle; 170 Britain on View/photolibrary.com; 171t AA/S Whitehorne; 171b AA/J Smith; 172 John Macpherson of Broombank Productions; 173 Colin Palmer Photography/Alamy; 174l Mary Evans Picture Library/Alamy; 174r John McKenna/Alamy; 175t AA/M Adelman; 175b Ashley Cooper/Alamy; 176 Alistair Dick/Alamy; 177l Christa Knijff/Alamy; 177r AA/R Weir; 178/179 D.G.Farquhar/Alamy; 179 BL Images Ltd/Alamy; 180 Holmes Garden Photos/Alamy; 181t Bill Bachmann/Alamy; 181bl Photoshot/Alamy; 181br AA/J Henderson; 182t David Robertson/Alamy; 182b BL Images Ltd/Alamy; 183 Jam World Images/Alamy; 184t AA/K Paterson; 184b Mary Evans Picture Library/Alamy; 185 David Robertson/Alamy; 186t AA/R Weir; 186b Photoshot/Alamy; 187t Mark Pink/Alamy; 187b David Kilpatrick/Alamy; 188t David Kilpatrick/Alamy; 188b AA/K Paterson; 189t Drumlanrig Castle and Country Estate, Thornhill, Dumfriesshire; 189b Drumlanrig Castle and Country Estate, Thornhill, Dumfriesshire; 190t AA/J Henderson; 190b Jim Henderson/Alamy; 191 South West Images Scotland/Alamy; 192 ImagesEurope/Alamy; 193t Peter Scholey/Alamy; 193b David Lyons/Alamy; 194l AA/J Beazley; 194r AA/K Blackwell; 195 AA/J Smith; 196l AA/J Henderson; 196r iWebbtravel/Alamy; 197l Tomobis/Alamy; 197r AA/S Whitehorne; 198/199 John McKenna/Alamy; 200 AA/K Blackwell; 201 Paul Melling/Alamy; 202t AA/R Weir; 202bl Adam Woolfitt/Robert Harding; 202br Adam Woolfitt/Robert Harding; 203 AA/R Coulam; 204l AA/E Ellington; 204r Richard Maschmeyer/Robert Harding; 205 David Lyons/Alamy; 206 Courtesy of Chivas Bros; 207 By kind permission of Nick McCann & Heritage House Group; 208 John Kelly/Alamy; 208/209 Angus McComiskey/Alamy; 210t AA/J Henderson; 210b Jim Henderson/Alamy; 211l Stephen Dorey - Bygone Images/Alamy; 211r AA/K Blackwell; 212tl Skyscan Photolibrary/Alamy; 212tr Danita Delimont Creative/Alamy; 212b David Kilpatrick/Alamy; 213l AA/K Blackwell; 213r 2d Alan King/Alamy; 214t AA/M Taylor; 214b Tony Wright/earthscapes/Alamy; 215t South West Images Scotland/Alamy; 215b South West Images Scotland/Alamy; 216t Daniel Sweeney (escapeimages.com)/Alamy; 216b AA/J Smith; 217 Steve Lindridge/Alamy; 218t AA/S Whitehorne; 218b Bailey-Cooper Photography/Alamy; 219t AA/K Blackwell; 219bl 2d Alan King/Alamy; 219cr AA/K Blackwell; 220t Mic Walker/Alamy; 220b Collpicto/Alamy; 221 AA/J Smith.

Every effort has been made to trace the copyright holders, and we apologise in advance for any accidental errors. We would be happy to apply the corrections in the following edition of this publication.